№ 15

THE SAMURAI OF VISHOGROD

THE SAMURAI OF VISHOGROD

The Notebooks of Jacob Marateck

retold by

Shimon and Anita Wincelberg

THE JEWISH PUBLICATION SOCIETY OF AMERICA
PHILADELPHIA

Portions of this book have appeared in Commentary, Hadassah Magazine, The Jerusalem Post, Jewish Frontier, Jewish Heritage, Jewish Horizon, The Jewish Observer, Moment, and National Jewish Monthly

To the memory of
Jacob and Bryna Marateck ע"ה

הנאהבים והנעימים בחייהם ובמותם לא נפרדו

*"Who were beloved and
pleasant in their lives, and
in death were not parted"*

Contents

During the early 1930s Jacob Marateck (1883–1950) resumed the journal he had begun during the Russo-Japanese War of 1904/05. At the time of his death he had filled a total of twenty-eight notebooks, none of which had he had the opportunity to revise and edit for publication in English.

This volume is drawn from the first sixteen notebooks, and the nineteen stories that follow were translated, edited, and, wherever necessary, "retold" by us, sometimes separately, sometimes in collaboration, during the years 1955 to 1975.

We would like to express our indebtedness to our sister, Mrs. Edith Marateck Feigenbaum, who initially translated most of these notebooks from Yiddish.

Our job also was greatly facilitated by our friend Rebbetzin Fayge Wasserman (of Yeshivah Or Elchonon in Los Angeles), who, over a period of years, prepared a complete Yiddish typescript from the handwritten original.

A. M. W.
S. W.

THE SAMURAI OF VISHOGROD

Introduction to
a Nickel Notebook

I still have the first notebook. I think I bought it from a peddler at the railroad station in Harbin, probably to keep some kind of record of my adventures. The date on the opening page reads, "August, 1903, Harbin, China," which of course is incorrect; it was 1904, and more likely September.

But I see that after a dozen pages (where I had written a poem whose only merit was that it rhymed and some "history" which showed mainly how little we knew of what was going on) the notebook began to be put to more practical uses—for letters, messages, cigarette paper. This is not really surprising, since we found ourselves almost immediately caught up in our army's headlong retreat across the frozen wastes of Manchuria. Also, I suppose, my curiosity was pretty much limited to whether our end would come from freezing or starvation, from Japanese artillery or from Chinese bandits, and whether it would be today or tomorrow (or, as we say more gracefully in our prayer for the New Year, "who in his time and who not in his time, who by fire and who by water, who by the sword and who by wild beasts, who by hunger and who by thirst . . .").

Only now that I am forty-seven years of age and suddenly have too much time on my hands do I feel moved to begin again, having in the twenty-seven-year interim been sidetracked by this and that. To begin with, the war itself (between Russia and Japan). Afterwards, finding it no longer possible to relapse into being my parents' child, I returned to Warsaw and once more became involved with the Jewish revolutionary movement, both as a kind of labor organizer and when necessary, I'm sorry to say, as what today you would call a "terrorist"—though I ask you to remember that Jews, not without reason, are known as "the merciful children of the merciful," and the only people in Warsaw with whom I ever engaged in a gun battle were the pimps of the Warsaw underworld. These wretched creatures not only preyed on the Jewish quarter, but also bought immunity for themselves and their merchandise by acting as informers for the czarist secret police. To whom, in fact, I was eventually betrayed. And so quickly and casually did they condemn me to death that my family would have known nothing about it to this day if it had not been for the totally miraculous intervention of a young lady who happened to be passing in the street, of whom I will have more to say in due course.

Having cheated the firing squad—for the second time—I spent the next seven months in sixteen different prisons or prison camps, until finally I escaped from the most desolate of them all, somewhere in the vastness of Siberia, with my friend G., who had been known in Warsaw as the King of Thieves but here, with no one to steal from, seemed somewhat out of his element.

Our escape led, in a curious way, to several unexpected months of almost unbearable luxury in the home of a young Siberian Jewish millionaire, to whom I had once lent fifty rubles to get home when we were in the army: bread cast upon the waters. But my friend's exquisite wife proved in the end to have the kind of problem which can sour the best of marriages, and, to evade the temptation which once had sorely tested our father Joseph, I finally cut short my fairy-tale existence and returned to

Warsaw, where at last I made the acquaintance of the girl, Bryna Migdal, who the year before had unknowingly saved me from being shot to death.

Married, with two children, but in sudden danger of being conscripted for a second time, I was obliged to travel alone to America, a road already pioneered by my brother Berel. Abruptly cut off from my family by the [First] World War, I was reunited with my wife and surviving daughter only after nine long years.

Now, blessed by the Almighty with a loving family and almost every talent except that for making money (not as a grocer, and not as a fishman, and not as a writer for the Yiddish press, and not shoveling snow or driving a beer truck, and certainly not as a synagogue president), I find, thanks to the Depression, the leisure to return, as though it were yesterday, to Vishogrod, from which (as the Almighty told our father Abraham, "Go *by yourself*, from your land, and from your birthplace, and from your father's house") my father, peace upon him, sent me at the age of twelve to learn at the yeshivah in Plinsk. But within a week I escaped from there like a thief in the night, believing, as I still do, that no Jew should be expected to fast more than two days a week.

Finally at thirteen, unable to learn a suitable craft in Vishogrod, I followed my older brother Mordechai to the great modern metropolis of Warsaw, where, I'd been told, one had only to turn a kind of screw in the wall to make water come pouring out. Here I too began, as an apprentice baker, that sorrowful trade which tradition then seemed to have reserved solely for runaways and delinquents.

But I soon worked my way up in the world until, at eighteen, being too strong and adventurous to consider self-mutilation, I was duly conscripted into "Fonya's"* army, where, in the name of Jewish honor, I was careful never to raise a hand against a Russian or Ukrainian comrade which did not result in at least one of us being hauled off to the hospital.

*Fonya, our name for Russians, being a diminutive of Ivan (Vanya), sometimes, for emphasis, expanded to "Fonya *gonnef*" (Fonya thief).

In the course of my military service I managed also to acquire several medals (including one for dancing), served for a time in the Czar's bodyguard, and had my first taste of armed combat (robbing some Chinese bandits of their food), and presently learned that, no matter how terrible it is for *anyone* to be in the midst of a war, it's a hundred times worse to be on the losing side.

Among our army's lesser crimes was its failure (possibly deliberate) to forward the letters we wrote to our families. Those who could write. As a result, the only news about us which trickled back was by way of those wounded who were lucky enough to be evacuated. It was in this manner that my family back home learned I was dead, causing my poor parents (for a *second* time), to sit *shiva* for me.

1. The Reluctant Wedding

When I say poor, I don't necessarily mean in a material sense, at least not to begin with. Although while I was growing up my father was as prosperous as a righteous man in *this* world—that is to say, he had about as much money as a Jew has pigs—that was not how he began life, for my father's father was the richest man in his town, being the only Jew permitted to supply the local Russian fortress with scrap metal, which he transported up the Vistula in his own fleet of barges.

Consequently, Shloime Zalman, my father, was raised in such princely comfort that, when he had to go to *cheder*, a short distance away, he was driven in a coach drawn by two horses. But since man, as we know, is incomplete until male and female are joined together, this made it only natural that at fourteen my father should one day without warning find himself betrothed to Rachel, daughter of Reb Shmuel Schlossberg, a ship's chandler and lumberman in nearby Novydvar, who herself had just attained the ripe age of thirteen.

The arrangements were of course made directly between the parents. After all, what did children know about a serious business like married life? The decision, in fact, was to hold the wedding that same year, before the two principals aged any further and possibly got ideas of their own.

Never, of course, did it enter my dear grandparents' heads that the way they raised their son might have left him insufficiently prepared to cope with future hardships, not to mention early marriage.

Fortunately, Reb Shmuel had committed himself not only to a generous dowry, but also to provide food and shelter for husband and wife "in perpetuity." So, as you can see, there was absolutely nothing to worry about.

Ten days before the appointed time for the wedding, the bride's entourage came gliding down the Vistula on their own ship, entertained by a Russian orchestra of (it was said) no less than sixty-four pieces, and a conductor from Vienna. They were met at the dock by the groom's family and, led by the band like an arriving circus or a military parade, the procession made its way to the marketplace. The shock waves from all this commotion not only jolted our own sleepy community, but shook up all the neighboring towns as well.

In accordance with tradition, the wedding was accompanied by a seven-day feast for the poor. At every meal sacks full of coins were distributed, not only by the groom's father, but separately by his mother as well, who like Abraham's wife, was known as "Our Mother Sarah," for she gave not only with a full hand, but also with a full heart.

Like my father, Rachel, the bride, also had known nothing whatever about these plans for her future, until people had suddenly descended upon her and fitted her for new clothes. What excitement, to be dressed so much better than all her girl friends! Once she learned, however, that she was to be *married*, she became intensely curious to know who her groom would be. But, being a properly modest girl, she was ashamed to ask. And since she didn't ask, nobody bothered to tell her. Why tell a child about such things? Once under the *chupah*, she'd have time enough to find out.

But now, as the time came to lead the bride under the canopy, she suddenly balked. (Now, if such a thing happened in our day, it would be easy enough to imagine some cause. Perhaps the groom, after having sworn eternal love to her, had been found kissing another girl in some dark corner. Or, having brought his betrothed home from the theater, had been seen at an ice cream parlor with another; or things of that sort. But in those days, of course such occurrences were completely unheard of. And besides, the bride and groom didn't even know each other. So how did she know she wouldn't like him?) After great difficulty, they discovered what was the matter. Rachel wasn't in the mood to go out into the street because it was drizzling outside, and she was afraid of getting spots on her beautiful new silk dress.

The way my father's father told it, he had trouble with his candidate, too. Shloime Zalman absolutely did not want to be married that day. He, too, wanted to know why they couldn't wait a few days until the weather cleared up. They finally had to shout at him that this whole affair wasn't any of his business, he had nothing to say about it, that he was still a little snotnose of a boy, and when his elders told him to go, his job was not to argue but to go.

After a good deal of aggravation in both houses, the ceremony finally did take place as scheduled, and for seven days things were doing, as they say, "on tables and benches." Afterwards, the carpet of white linen on which the bride and groom walked from their homes to the synagogue was given to the poor, who used it to make shirts for themselves. This signified that the festivities were over.

My mother's parents now prepared to return home on their private ship, taking with them the groom, to be eternally provided for according to contract—not only himself and his bride, but also their children and children's children. In return for which all my father had to do was study Torah and live with his wife.

At this point, fresh complications arose. The new husband, who had meanwhile turned fifteen, burst into tears. He didn't want to go away with strangers. He wanted to stay home with his friends. When the Maratecks came aboard to say goodbye to their daughter-in-law, she became bashful and hid in a barrel. The result was that my father's mother had to go along until the boy accustomed himself to his new situation. She said, "What can you do? After all, he's only a child. . . ."

But even with his mother there, each day, when the Schlossberg family sat down to dinner, my father did everything imaginable to avoid sitting next to his wife. It was said of them that "their love burned like a wet rag."

My mother was equally reluctant to abandon her childhood. Often, her husband would come home from the house of study to find her playing in the yard. Hearing his approach, she would run hastily into the house, leaving her womanly head covering in the sand.

Time passed. Gradually Shloime Zalman was able to live with his wife without having his mother around. The young pair matured, grew to love each other, and had children of their own, including me. But, as we know, while we live in exile, Jewish wealth is as durable as smoke. Despite the marriage contract which guaranteed my father "sustenance in perpetuity," the Schlossberg fortunes took a sharp turn for the worse, and my father quite suddenly found himself obliged to provide not only for his growing family, but for his in-laws as well.

In later years my parents would point to their own lives as proof that true love comes only *after* marriage. In fact, they believed this so firmly that they tried not less than seventeen times to arrange matches for *me*. Finally, at the age of twenty-seven, I put a stop to negotiations for an "heiress" with red hair and a temper, and married the girl who, back in Warsaw, had saved me from being shot.

2. The Samurai of Vishogrod and the Very Small Pogrom

One of the legendary heroes of my childhood was Yonah the messenger, at that time already in his sixties, yet a man of such vigor still that I can hardly begin to picture what he must have been like in his youth.

Being a hero, of course, at least in our corner of the world, was not exactly a full-time job, nor, even on a part-time basis, a profession on which a man could feed his family. And so, in his everyday existence, Yonah was simply a part of our "postal service," which, in its own way, was as curious a feature of Vishogrod life as the man himself.

For ordinary mail we had an ordinary letter carrier, a man named Yudel, who could neither read nor write, and therefore cruel tongues, quite overlooking his more serious infirmities, called him "Blind Yudel." But we also had two special messengers available for the delivery of telegrams, money, or urgent communications which, you will be surprised to know, often happened more than once a year.

Of course, even the regular mailman came so rarely that one day, when my brother Avrohom and I were locked in alone in the house and heard a sharp knock on the door, we crawled under the covers in terror and, unaccustomed to the sudden warmth, fell asleep. (What were we doing in bed in the first place? It saved coal.)

The next day, in case evil spirits should come knocking again, our mother stayed home with us, keeping warm by sitting huddled over a bucket of live coals between her feet and looking, may she forgive me, less like a mother than like a pile of rags.

Sure enough, in the midst of howling winds, there was that knocking again, only embellished this time with a dry, ghostly cough.

My mother shrank with fear, and my brother and I covered our heads with the blanket. Only Itteleh, the butcher's wife, who was visiting with us, held on to her wits. She picked up a cleaver, went to the door, and screamed, "Demon! Unclean Spirit! Back to your resting place!" (As you can see, in Vishogrod we knew how to deal with the Powers of Darkness.)

Only this time, a plaintive voice outside replied, "I'm Yudel the postman. Let me in, I'm freezing."

As it turned out, the letter he'd been trying to deliver to us for the past week was actually for someone else. But no one, of course, held that against him—an illiterate Jew, after all, being as uncommon and as deserving of pity as any other kind of cripple.

Yudel got no salary from the government. Recipients paid him two kopeks for a postcard and three for a sealed letter, and sometimes even four, if it came all the way from Warsaw. A letter from Warsaw normally took several weeks, during which time Ignatz, the Pole who drove the postal wagon with its two dying horses, plodded staunchly through oceans of mud and somehow crossed rivers largely lacking in of such conveniences as bridges or ferries. Thus, who could blame Ignatz if sometimes he decided to make a little stop for recuperation at a wayside inn, empty a bottle or two, dally with one of his mistresses, and, as often as not, return to Warsaw without delivering the mail because he'd forgotten in which direction he was headed?

Anyway, when God helped and the mail finally did arrive, Reb Yudel would put on his uniform, consisting of a shapeless cap with a green band, proudly pin his father's medal (from the Russo-Turkish War) over his breast, and commence to march (that is, marching with one foot and dragging the other) down the main street with an air befitting a man who was, for the moment, not only an arm of the government, but also entitled to the respect due the son of a decorated soldier; for Vishogrod, like any other little Jewish town, not only had its share of otherworldly talmudists and starving merchants, but its heroes as well. Of whom, more in a moment.

Now since Yudel, through no fault of his own, almost invariably misdelivered the mail, some well-meaning people suggested that my father, who was at that time without employment, and not only could read and write Yiddish and Hebrew but also knew Polish, Russian, and a bit of German, should become the town's letter carrier.

Others, however, quickly pointed out that the job had not only been in Yudel's family for generations, but why should *he* be penalized for the undeserved misfortune of being illiterate? The question actually was academic, because my father would never have violated the biblical command against trespassing on another's territory for any amount of money. He was, in fact, far too proud a man to have accepted such a menial position *for pay;* nor would my mother have wanted him to. (When there was no hot food in the house for *Shabbos,* and we seemed in imminent danger of having one of our neighbors share their meal with us, my mother would leave a large pot of water boiling in the kitchen Friday afternoon, so that no passerby, God forbid, might suspect the Maratecks were going hungry.)

But what was to be done? People *did* like to get their own mail, even though, more often than not, it was bound to contain only more bad news. Didn't a letter go through enough suffering and uncertainty *before* it reached town without also being abandoned to the incompetence of Blind Yudel?

But leave it to Jews to find a solution. A clearinghouse was established in the synagogue and, by common agreement, whenever anyone received a letter addressed to someone else, instead of returning it to the uncertain fate of Reb Yudel's dubious mail pouch and perhaps hurting his feelings besides, he would bring it with him to evening prayers and place it on the pulpit. Any time a few letters accumulated, my father would mount the pulpit after the final *kaddish* and read off the correct names. This satisfied all factions, although of course it overlooked the fact that this brought my father not one kopek closer to making a living.

But what about telegrams, packages, rabbinical documents, or letters with money inside? For this responsible job we had, as I said, not merely one messenger available, but two.

The lower-grade "special deliveries" were made by Moishka, a little man with a scraggly, sulfurous beard and, between us, a man of middling intelligence, that is, neither a great genius nor a small fool. (They tell that once he was sent with an urgent letter from Vishogrod to Novydvar, an all-night journey, and he came back with the letter undelivered because the man to whom it had been addressed was still sleeping when he arrived.)

But the other messenger, the only one who was trusted with money, or with parcels of sufficient value to attract robbers, was Yonah, known even to our gentiles as "Yonah the Iron Man." Yonah, although already blessed with enough grandsons to make up a quorum in at least two synagogues, was, not to exaggerate, another Samson. Perhaps not quite as strong or as violent, but, on the other hand, also the last man in the world who would have let a Philistine wench lead him around by the nose.

They used to tell how one day Eisenberg the lumber dealer sent Yonah to Warsaw with an astronomical amount of money to put into the bank there. Yonah tied on his two big bags of money with a rope, tucked his earlocks into his cap (after all, though he surely wasn't *ashamed* of his earlocks, why go out of your way to look for a fight with some ignorant peasant, when you were being paid to save your energies for quite another sort of trouble?), and, carrying the bag with his *tallis* and *tefillin*, two loaves of bread, and a dozen onions, set off on foot, armed with nothing but a stout stick.

Anyway, while he was pacing along briskly through a dark forest in the middle of the night (sleep, of course, being out of the question), refreshing himself with a piece of bread and onion, and keeping himself company by reciting the Psalms in a voice as pure as thunder, he was halted by an armed robber. What we Americans would call a holdup man. Carrying an immense revolver, which seemed to be fairly bursting with large lead bullets eager to be discharged. He told Yonah to hand over all the money he was carrying, or else he would shoot him down on the spot, absolutely without mercy, like a dog.

Fortunately for Yonah, the bandit was a Jew (for what other kind of bandit would even *talk* about such a thing as mercy?), so that it was possible to discuss the matter in a civilized way.

Yonah explained that he was certainly ready to hand over the money. After all, it wasn't his. But there was his reputation to consider. Knowing him as a fearless and powerful man, his employer surely would refuse to believe that Yonah would have given up such a sum of money without at least some *signs* of a struggle.

What better way to prove that he'd been overpowered by a man with a gun than to be able to display an actual bullet hole in his coat? It was, after all, a small enough favor to ask for the sake of preserving one's reputation as an honest man.

The bandit, being, as I said, Jewish, understood Yonah's predicament perfectly and sent a large, well-aimed bullet through Yonah's coattail, which was accommodatingly open.

You know the outcome. Jewish bandits in Poland didn't have six-shooters. The demonstration bullet had emptied the gun. At which point, Yonah felt it safe to deal the foolish bandit a small tap—which left him lying unconscious with a generously bleeding nose.

So Yonah continued on his way, loudly resuming his recital of Psalms where he'd left off, while the poor bandit, once he recovered consciousness, yelled after him in deep reproach that he never would have believed a God-fearing man capable of playing such a low trick on a fellow Jew. (And, though I now suspect that the whole story is pure legend, this was at least the sort of thing they *told* about him. What I mean is, true or not, do they tell such stories about *you?*)

Of course, all this is merely to set the stage, as it were, for the story I *meant* to tell you. In our neighboring town of Bazenova, a rumor had gone around that on the coming market day "a little pogrom" was going to take place. I don't know how it was where *you* came from, but in our part of Poland, all rumors had one characteristic in common: the bad ones were never false.

Now by a "little pogrom" I take it that they meant it was to be essentially a *civilian* undertaking, without cavalry support or firearms, or that sort of thing. Still, for a stallkeeper, with only a basket of eggs standing between him and total starvation, even an *infinitesimal* pogrom was a thing, given a choice, one would prefer to do without. No such choice being available, a delegation was dispatched hastily to our Rabbi with a plea for help. That is to say, a plea for Yonah.

Now on market days, even in the best of times, the hordes of peasants let loose in Bazenova were something of a hazard. And not only did the people of Bazenova have no one fit to mention in the same breath with our Yonah (while we in Vishogrod actually were blessed with a number of other good Jewish ruffians as well), but their entire police force consisted of two men, the younger of whom would never see seventy again, while the other gendarme, when he had to go up one step to enter a store for the policeman's customary reason the world over (that is, with his hand open in front of him), a kindly passerby would have to seize his elbow and give him a little boost. Upon the shoulders of these two ferocious guardians of the law rested the protection of Bazenova's Jews against a mob of drunken, bloodthirsty peasants.

On the other hand, it must be admitted that Bazenova's Jews never dreamt of protesting this situation, as it is a well-known fact that the older and feebler a policeman gets, the less energy he has left over for hitting Jews.

So our Rabbi ordered that a dozen of our "men of valor," under Yonah's leadership, were to drive out Tuesday morning and lend the benefit of their experience to Bazenova's embattled Jews.

(In later years, when my wanderings took me to Japan, which I'll tell you about another time, I found that this sort of arrangement used to be traditional there, too, although the defenders *they* used, called samurai, got *paid* for fighting, and I never could understand why, since the Japanese villagers were not Jews, anyone should want to attack them.)

So on Monday night, the eve of market day, Yonah and his men set out, with God's help and the Rabbi's blessings, in two wagons drawn by teams of horses furnished by our town's richest Jews. As people in those days were usually too poor to own rifles or machine guns, their entire arsenal consisted of stones, clubs, and fists.

If I go into such detail over an incident at which, as far as I can remember, I was not even present, it is perhaps to explain why, much as I loved my father, the person I most aspired to resemble when I grew up was Yonah, our "Samurai of Vishogrod."

They stopped overnight at a very decent inn on the outskirts of Bazenova, and on Tuesday morning, Yonah and his band, after putting away a respectable breakfast of roast duckling and plum brandy, betook themselves, glowing with good humor, to the Market Square, looking to all the world like jolly merchants out for a nice bargain in a horse or a bushel of potatoes.

The market was already crowded with peasants, and everyone, with the possible exception of the policemen, could sense that something was in the wind.

Yonah sized up the situation in a moment. Like a good general, he divided up his little army into four companies, so that they could never all be surrounded at the same time, for the techniques of street fighting in those days were already beginning to outgrow the primitive methods of an earlier age.

Yonah himself set up his command post in the attic of Shmuel the scribe. From here he was able to survey the entire square, and gauge the exact moment at which an accumulation of "normal" incidents would flare up into a concerted, if still reasonably small, pogrom. As a strategist, he knew the importance of not putting your cards on the table too early.

Here and there, little incidents had already begun to erupt. Some loaves of bread snatched from a baker. A basket of eggs robbed from Sheindel the midwife. In the widow Yetta's little store, some peasants broke the windows and emptied a sack of flour. When she protested, they beat her and told her that today they meant to finish off every Jew in town and take over their property, because the priest had told them Sunday morning that everything the Jews owned had been stolen from the peasants anyway.

Thus far, as you can see, everything was quite normal, and someone less shrewd than Yonah might have suspected the whole thing had been a false alarm. But he knew from experience that a Polish peasant, unlike, say, a Ukrainian, has to work himself up to a real pogrom by gradual stages. And so, after listening cold-bloodedly to the dispatches coming in all morning, it took a little while before he decided finally that the time had come for his men to go back to the wagons and, in a manner of speaking, arm themselves. Favored by nearly all of them were clubs of plum-wood, hard as iron.

However, since it was close to lunchtime now, and there was no telling how soon they would get to eat, they digressed long enough to take aboard another round of schnapps. Following this, with the cry, "Jews, for *kiddush ha-shem!*" Yonah committed his little army.

By this time, the pogrom had erupted in earnest. Goods were being looted by the armful, and even failure to protest didn't save stallkeepers, women and children included, from being beaten right and left. The noise was fantastic and the entire market boiled with flailing arms and clubs, collapsing stands and flying things, from bloody feathers to paving blocks.

It took Yonah and his four companies some time to fight their way into the eye of the storm. By this time, the peasants had been gripped by the excitement of the thing, and their leaders were no longer bent so much on plunder as on the pure joy of bloodshed. Yonah himself had entered the market barehanded. Up to now, in fact, he had even retained his customary air of calm good humor. Until he saw one of his men go down with a spurting head, struck from behind by a paving stone. At this, he leaped up at an approaching wagon whose peasant driver had been running cheerfully over a row of stalls. He seized the peasant by the throat and flung him into the crowd. Then, with a voice like thunder, he identified himself as Yonah the messenger from Vishogrod, and warned the peasants to clear out at once.

Those who knew him or had heard of his reputation instantly took their legs on their shoulders and fled. But the majority simply laughed at him.

Yonah, still determined to give them one more chance (since by our law, even the owner of a rampaging ox is entitled to one warning), jumped down, tore the back wheels off the wagon, and lifted up the axle. However, those peasants who had remained were, by this time, far too flushed with vodka and thirst for blood to be impressed even by this performance. And so he began laying about him with the axle of the wagon, and his little army, heartened by his example, contributed their own modest share in his wake.

Within a few minutes, the Market Square was a wilderness. Some of the peasants who were still on their feet escaped in such haste, they left horses, wagons, and even livestock behind them.

By midafternoon, the Bazenova "hospital," that is, the Russian doctor's barn, overflowed with casualties. There were countless fractures, but no dead. Jews, as I may have mentioned earlier, are children of mercy. The defenders, too, carried back their share of wounds, both major and minor, but all agreed that the whole expedition had been very worthwhile.

And who, by the way, do you suppose turned out to have been one of the first casualties? It was the younger of the two ancient gendarmes, who had stopped half a brick with the back of his head while running away.

That was not quite the end of it. A few weeks later, an investigating commission arrived from the office of the provincial governor. Yonah, his fellow "samurais," and several dozen peasants were placed under arrest, on some trumped-up charge like disturbing the peace, or "causing willful and malicious damage to cattle, property, and subjects of the Czar."

But they were never brought to trial. The peasants were far too frightened for their lives to testify against Yonah. He, for his part, pressed no charges; he probably felt that they had already been punished adequately, and besides, the only pogroms in which the governor could be expected to take a meaningful interest were those he had incited himself.

But for as long as I can remember after that, not even a *very* small pogrom ever took place again in Bazenova. The peasants must have passed on to their children and even their children's children the wisdom of not starting up with such a barbaric people as the Jews.

3. Eating Days

As I said, my father, reared in luxury, was not in the least equipped to struggle for his own existence. Whatever he touched fell buttered side down. He had no aptitude for skilled labor, and he was not shrewd enough for trade. All he really knew how to do properly was rock over a page of Talmud, which in those days was not a very profitable occupation. That is to say, all the wisdom with which he crammed his head was not enough to put bread on his family's table. It finally became impossible to keep the family together any longer. One by one, as they grew to be twelve or thirteen, his children tore out into the world, leaving their impoverished home behind them forever.

Soon only my brother Chayim and I and Avrohom, the youngest, were left.

Then Chayim, too, decided to go. He had become possessed with the crazy idea that he wanted to be a great scholar. For this, he was willing to suffer exile and worse. He didn't want to learn a trade, he only wanted to go on with his studies, even after he was thirteen. Since our parents could not support him, he went off to other villages, where he kept alive by "eating days." That is, the *shammes* of the synagogue would find a number of householders, each of whom would be responsible for his meals one day a week. Along with other boys like himself, he slept in the synagogue.

Of course, no great ceremony was made about sleeping. After all, if a boy was going to learn day and night, what did he need a bed for? So that if, late at night, a boy became sleepy in the middle of his studies, he simply lay down on a bench, put his arms under his head, and snored for a few hours.

When the worshippers came at dawn to say Psalms, one of them was sure to yell, "Chayim! Time to get up and learn. Do you want to sleep all day?" And they weren't too gentle about it, either. One would tug at his arm, another would pull at his leg, and a third might shake the bench. Before long, the boy was bound to realize there was no profit in idleness, and return to his studies.

Should he, however, take time to scratch himself, or still yawn sleepily, a cry arose, "Heathen! Quick, wash your hands and say Psalms."

And what boy, feeling himself guilty of sleeping in a holy place, would dare to protest?

At any rate, far worse than the lack of sleep was the lack of food. A boy who managed to get fed every day of the week was considered unusually fortunate.

Chayim clung to his studies though he turned, as the saying goes, black with privation. (He ultimately wound up as a *shochet* in Scranton, Pennsylvania, and continued to study for the rest of his days.)

But why am I telling you all this? Because, inspired by Chayim's example, I, too, decided to become a scholar. I, too, ate "days." But I lasted only one week. And this is why.

The first day I was scheduled to eat at Reb Shlomo T.'s, a prosperous householder in a neighboring village. I don't know how long I paced up and down in front of his house and struggled with myself to go in. I was not only painfully shy, but mortified at the thought of appearing like a beggar. Finally, though I was well aware that if I was going to be too ashamed to eat "days" I would surely die of hunger, I set out on the long walk back to the *beth hamidrash.*

I didn't know what to do. I only knew that I wanted to be brave and learned like Chayim, and that I didn't want to go back home.

So I continued to study as though I had eaten. But when afternoon arrived, I was so faint with hunger, I suddenly burst into tears. At that, an old Psalm-sayer came over, found out the reason for my crying, and gave me a good talking to.

"Where there is no bread, there is no Torah," he said. He took me by the hand and led me all the way back to the home to which I had been assigned. To the lady of the house he said, "This child is to eat here, and he is ashamed to come in." She was a kindly, energetic woman in a *shaitel,* who gave me a wonderful lunch and told me to be sure and come back for dinner. I did. That was Sunday.

Monday I ate at Reb Nathan S.'s, though again I had to be led there and introduced.

My "Tuesday" was a miser, who begrudged food even to himself. He had agreed to feed a boy one day a week, but only because the congregation had shamed him into it. When I arrived, my host grumpily pointed out my portion to me, a plate containing a piece of bread so thin you could see through it, a small herring, and a cold glass of tea without sugar.

I gulped down my meal through tears of embarrassment, and ran from the house. Then I heard my host calling after me, "Hey, boy!" I stopped. I thought he meant to give me something else to eat. But he only wanted to let me know that his wife was washing clothes that day and would not be cooking, so that I needn't come back for the evening meal.

Wednesday I was to eat at the home of a traveling peddler. But when I got there, the door was locked. My host was out of town. So that day I ate nothing. However, toward evening I was told that a woman was looking for me. I went outside, and she asked me if I was the boy from Vishogrod who was to have eaten at her house that day.

I told her I was, and she gave me something wrapped in paper. It was a piece of bread and herring. That way, I suppose, she could still feel she had fulfilled the *mitzvah* of feeding a yeshivah student for a day.

Thursday, it had been arranged for me to eat at the home of a wealthy man who had emigrated from Berlin. There I got so much to eat and drink, I was barely able to rise from the table. Later I learned that when the committee had first proposed to him that he give one of the students a "day" to eat, he appeared to be totally ignorant of the custom. He told them with a wink, "If the young man is an expert at eating 'days,' maybe he'll eat up Yom Kippur for me, so that I won't have to fast."

No big fuss was made over Friday, because, after all, on the Sabbath you ate three solid meals, two of them, as befits a Jew who on this day is the equal of a king, including both meat *and* fish. So Friday, until sunset, I went hungry.

But for the Sabbath meals I had been invited to the home of my father's friend, K., a Gerer Hasid, and if the food was meager, we compensated for it to a large extent by singing a great many *zmiros* with considerable fervor, as was the Gerer style.

Of course, *nowadays* when a child of poor parents grows up, thought is given to providing him with a trade. But in my father's time, although most of our parents, skilled or unskilled, worked long and hard to provide for their families, only one kind of "trade" really counted, and that was the advanced study of Torah and Talmud. This was not entirely as impractical as it may sound. There were rich Jews who wanted their sons to study with great scholars, and were willing to pay good salaries to get one as a private tutor. Sometimes one even heard that the tutor had gotten to marry the rich man's daughter.

So, with even such worldly rewards open to them, the children of the poor would spend years, decades, on the hard benches of study. As a result, they really could learn, but physically, many of them were so stunted from malnutrition and lack of fresh air and physical exercise, they looked almost tubercular, and their eyes and voices were without life or luster.

Looking then at my fellow students, they seemed to me, with their limp postures and downcast eyes, to resemble the soaked herrings on which they lived, and I suppose they left a powerful impression on me. I couldn't help thinking, "When I grow up, will I look like them?"

Right then I decided that if this were the price of becoming a scholar, then I would not be a scholar.

Accordingly, I got up early next morning and took my two shirts, the one with patches and the one with holes, and tied them up in a red bandanna. With the shirts I put a piece of bread I had saved from the Sabbath meal, and then I set out for home.

There was of course no thought of going by coach. That would have cost five gulden (about seventy-five cents), and my total fortune consisted of two gulden.

Upon leaving the village, the first thing I did was remove my boots. For two reasons. One, walking is easier without boots, and two, walking would wear them out. They had already been in the process of expiring for some time.

So I set off in the direction of Zakhrachin, where I hoped to spend the night at the home of my great-aunt, and from there might be able to afford the coach the rest of the way.

But I was a poor judge of distances. I walked on and on until hunger did not permit me to continue. Then I sat down under a tree, and began to open my bandanna.

The piece of bread, I remembered sadly, was very small, and my appetite was very large. I also realized that if I ate all the bread now, I would starve later, and if I ate half of it now, it would only wake up my appetite and then it would be even worse. I looked into the bandanna. The bread was gone.

Some miles back I had taken it out to decide whether or not to eat it then, and I probably hadn't tied the bandanna tight enough after I put it back. I assure you I felt worse than a person who has lost his entire fortune. (I know because later in life I had that experience, too.) Now I really began to feel faint, and soon found myself sobbing bitterly. I simply had no strength to go any further.

A peasant who was working in a nearby field heard me cry, and came over and asked me in Polish, "What's the matter, little boy?"

At first I did not want to say anything. How could a poor peasant help me? But he gently patted my head and asked me to tell him what was troubling me.

Still sobbing, I told him of my great misfortune with the piece of bread. The peasant nodded understandingly, took me by the hand and led me to his house. It was a one-room hut, with walls of limestone and a roof of straw. Hopefully, I stood by the door and waited for him to offer me a piece of bread. My soul seemed ready to expire from hunger. But again I was to be disappointed. After a long discussion with his wife, in some Polish dialect, the peasant took me by the hand once more, and had me get into his wagon.

After a short ride we arrived at a neighbor's house. Here I was immediately handed a chunk of fresh bread and a cup of water. You can imagine how I fell upon it. But I still didn't understand why the first peasant had not given me any bread himself, though I had seen some on his table, but instead had taken me to a neighbor whose house looked no richer than his own.

After I had eaten, he explained. His wife baked her bread with lard, while her neighbor baked hers with oil. That is, seeing I was a Jewish child, they had gone to all this trouble to keep me from eating forbidden food, thus, in their kindness, unwittingly observing the rabbinic interpretation of "You shall not cause the blind to stumble."

4. The Lean of the Land

You must not think that, even at thirteen, I would run away from yeshivah without some sort of plan in mind. Hard as things were among the people with whom I'd been assigned to "eating days," I had enough sense to know it was still a hundred times sweeter to starve among Jews than among strangers. But of course I preferred to do neither.

Sooner or later, I knew I would have to return and face my father, and try somehow to justify my running away. But, although my father was not an unreasonable man, I naturally hoped to delay that painful moment for as long as possible.

As a boy who had, for whatever childish reason, thrown away a precious opportunity to sit and learn, I knew I needn't count on any grand reception. I mean my father, while he had never begrudged his children anything within his power, also had a forceful way of expressing his disappointment, especially on those occasions when it seemed certain I was turning straight into a heathen —or that particular brand of heathen called *apikores,* literally, "epicurean"—which, in our town, seemed invariably to begin with skipping your afternoon prayers.

But, as I said, I had a plan. This was to put off going home until my father would be so happy merely to find me still alive, he might forget his disillusionment with me as a scholar. Mature as I was in other ways, it never occurred to me what terrible anxiety or grief parents might feel when their child disappears.

Meanwhile, I was still with the Polish peasant couple who had given me bread. And since evening was already approaching once more, and traveling at night was unsafe even for a boy whose very shoes weren't worth stealing, they told me I could stay overnight, and tomorrow the Jewish peddler would stop by and surely take me along to Zakhrachin.

They made a bed of hay for me in the stable, and in the morning when I went in to thank them and to say goodbye, the peasant's wife instantly ladled out a glass of milk for me. But since her ladle might also have been used for soups, I declined. I wasn't being especially heroic. After all, by nightfall I was bound to have reached Zakhrachin, and there my Aunt Malkah would feed me.

Afraid the peddler might slow me down, I set out alone. By the time I reached Zakhrachin, it was well after midnight. Nowhere in the black, silent streets did I see a living creature of whom I could ask directions to my aunt's house. It was too cold to stand still or lie down, which left me with nothing to do but roam the streets like a stray dog.

The sky seemed smeared with mud as thick as that which clung to my legs, as I wandered and blundered up and down the twisting, narrow, slippery alleys in my torn, bedraggled boots, in which the water entered in front and came out in the back. And still no glimmer of a soul one could accost for directions. I may have forgotten to mention it was also raining, not mere drops but solid sheets of water.

By now, I had reached a degree of overall misery which made me curse my greed for daily meals, my fear of going home, and my general childish adventurousness, when suddenly I saw two men with sticks running in my direction from the bottom of the road.

Their uphill progress had, to me, a kind of floating, dreamlike lethargy, because plainly they could run only as fast as the mud would allow. But of course I became frightened and, at the same nightmarishly slow pace, tried to pick up my feet and run away from them.

At this, I heard them shout in Polish, "Stop the thief! Catch him," and other such words of encouragement, which only made me run even harder. Until at a crossroad, not sure of which way to turn, I overshot my balance and ended up face down in a large, rapidly deepening pool of mud.

My two pursuers caught up and dragged me out. They seemed as angry as though I had tried to cheat them by drowning myself. One of them, who had the brow of an ox, wanted to introduce his stick to my head on the spot. I cowered and cringed in anticipation. But the other watchman stopped him, shrewdly pointing out there was no profit in beating me unconscious until I had told them what I'd been stealing.

I told them indignantly that I was not a thief. I'd come here to visit my great-aunt, Malkah Marateck, but didn't know where to find her in the dark. Even as I spoke, I could see it didn't sound like much of a story.

But the smaller of the two watchmen, the one who'd kept me from having my skull bashed in, now turned out to be a Jew. And, if you'll forgive my mentioning it, he was the one with some sense.

He subdued his partner with the ingenious proposal that they march me straight over to my Aunt Malkah's house, wake her up, and ask her if she knew me. It was a brilliant plan but, from my point of view, it had one flaw. As I may have neglected to mention earlier, my aunt had never seen me before in her life. How would she be able, in the middle of the night, to verify that I was her relative and not some thief?

With each man clinging to one of my elbows the way a bridegroom is led to the canopy, they marched me directly to my aunt's house.

The Jewish watchman pounded on the door. No response.

With every second, I could see the other watchman regaining some hope that he would get to beat me senseless after all. My soul was ready to evaporate, before my uncle inside finally found a match, lit the lamp, and unbolted the door.

The watchmen pushed me into the one-room house, shone the lamp in my face, and asked my uncle and aunt if they knew this boy.

Both unhesitatingly said no.

The Polish watchman cried triumphantly, "Aha! I knew at once he's a thief." Since the ceiling was too low for him to raise his stick, he started to drag me back outside.

But I clutched on to the other watchman, and stammered to the old people that I was Yankele Marateck, the son of Shloime Zalman, from Vishogrod.

My aunt, it now turned out, had not seen my parents for a mere eighteen years. But finally out of some dusty corner of her mind she recalled that she did indeed have relatives in Vishogrod. Only what was *I* doing here in the middle of the night?

"I'm on my way back home from the yeshivah," I said as casually as I could. "And I thought I'd stop and visit my relatives."

My uncle, who'd been silent all this time, now showed himself to be not such an oaf, after all. He said, "Yes relative, no relative, the boy doesn't look to me like a thief. What thief would come looking for *us?* Fix up a place for him to sleep. Relative or not, he's still a Jewish child."

The Polish watchman, deeply disappointed, let go of my arm, and they both left. My aunt at once made up a bed for me out of an old overcoat and shawl, with a straw sack for a pillow, and her skirt for a blanket.

When I woke up in the morning, I could hear them discussing me. My aunt now recalled that, among my parents' eight children, there was a boy named Yankel who now would be just about my age. In which case I was telling the truth.

My uncle gently scolded, "Why didn't you remember that last night? You might have given him something to put in his mouth. He probably hadn't eaten all day." In this, of course, he was absolutely correct, and he could have added most of the previous day as well.

My aunt, now penitent for her lack of hospitality, told her husband to take me with him to *shul*, and by the time we returned from morning prayers she would have a feast ready for me. "Black bread there is. And I'll cook cabbage and potatoes, in water from the river. I'm going right now to fetch the water."

While this might not sound so very appetizing to you, I found out later that in Zakhrachin the water you got from the well was bitter, while water from the river was a kind of delicacy, reserved only for honored guests.

Meanwhile I'd begun to stir. At once my aunt ran over. "Look at him, our Yankele, how handsome he looks, just like his father." She hugged me and kissed me, until my uncle told her she would do me a lot more good with a glass of milk.

Returning half an hour later from *shul*, I really did find a large meal awaiting me, and indeed the river water did not seem to have hurt the taste of the potatoes.

After breakfast, I reluctantly made ready to continue on my homeward journey. Not that I suddenly had acquired sense enough to take pity on my parents. But, like a child, I simply felt homesick. Of course, my aunt wouldn't hear of it. I had to stay at least a couple of days. And since, as I said, I was not *really* thirsting to face my father's disappointment in me, I wasn't too hard to persuade.

In fact, I might have stayed with them to this day, but for one thing.

Now, here in Columbus's country, where it is fashionable to lose ourselves in nostalgic reflections about the beauty, piety, and simplicity of life in what is now patronizingly called the *shtetl*, those largely hideous little towns and villages where anticipations of massacre were relieved only by the more immediate fears of starvation, the fashion also requires that we indulge in fantasies about the magical sweetness of our grandmothers' cookery.

But in this, as in other things, it's good to keep a sense of proportion. And, as I remember to this day, even for someone as starved as I, who had fervently appreciated my aunt's first breakfast, it didn't take me long to realize that my wonderful, hospitable Aunt Malkah, may she forgive me, was also one of the world's most terrible cooks.

Now I readily admit that, when it came to food, my standards might have been a little spoiled. That was because, when my mother cooked a perfectly ordinary meal, potatoes with farfel, chick-peas with farfel, or even, bless His Name, a little piece of meat, it seemed to me that the odors hung over the neighborhood like a perfume.

In fact, there were few Jewish women in Poland who did not know, in their cooking, how to make something wonderful out of almost nothing (not to mention such necessary arts as how to "revive" a piece of meat that had gone bad). But among those few, my Aunt Malkah surely held a place of honor. How was it, I ask, that she managed, with the best will in the world, to take a perfectly innocent dish and transform it into something that made you gag like a Turk who had swallowed a chew of tobacco?

To begin with, there was the oven she used. It was a square hole in the wall with a chimney above it, and two bricks inside supporting a sheet of iron on which you placed the pot.

But, for at least half the year, the wood used to heat the pot usually was damp and wouldn't burn. For this my aunt had a remedy. She would wave her apron sharply up and down like a bellows until the fire caught. When the water finally boiled, and some of the food began to run over into the fire, and the room was choked with hissing black smoke, and you had to open the front door to let out the smell, *then* at least she knew the food was *cooking*.

Exactly how sanitary things were under those conditions depended largely upon the habits of the cook. There being, of course, no faucets, all water for cooking and drinking had to be hauled from the well or the river, and was kept in a barrel by the oven.

Beside it stood a tub for the dirty water. Now, you could tell a well-ordered household simply by the fact that there was usually a full barrel and an empty tub.

In my aunt's house, I must admit, it was often the reverse.

Under the circumstances, it was not terribly difficult to make a mistake. Once, I remember I got up at night, still half-asleep, burning with thirst, and ladled myself a drink. It turned out to be from the wrong container, and I remember the foul taste of it to this day. After that, I frequently wondered at mealtimes whether the same mistake hadn't been made by my aunt.

In her defense, I will say that since the oven was always swirling with ashes and soot, it was impossible to see what was going on inside the pot. If my aunt had stuck her head in to look, she merely would have blocked out what little light trickled into the room.

On the other hand, of course, when my mother fanned the fire with her apron, she first put a lid on the pot. My aunt didn't bother with such refinements, and thus invariably she managed to fan ashes, soot, dust, and even small fragments of coal into the pot. This was why her borsht, for example, always had the color of dark brown mud, with a flavor to match. (Luckily, my uncle was the sort of innocent who, as they say, "doesn't know borsht is red.")

My mother, after using a ladle, would place it on a board to dry. My aunt would rest it directly in the ashes. As a result, no matter what it was she cooked, the surface of it soon would be garnished with the same fine layer of burned wood, charcoal, and grit. And since she never had the patience to watch a pot, it would invariably boil over. At this, my aunt would snatch the ladle from the ashes, dip it in the barrel, and like a fireman, fling cold water into the boiling pot, whose contents soon began to simmer down obediently and, at the same time, to turn ashen gray.

Once she put a pot of water on for tea, and, while waiting for it to boil, went off to a neighbor's house. After a while, it began to bubble, and I took it off the fire and filled myself a glass. There were so many little leaves swimming around in it, I thought she had brewed it too strong. As I was adding water and sugar, my aunt returned and said, "Wait, I didn't put the tea in yet."

After a week of such cuisine, I had already forgotten my starvation of the week before, and much as I still dreaded going home, I realized I was in less fear of my father's wrath than of my aunt's cooking.

And yet, long after I had left them, Aunt Malkah and her husband continued to live to a healthy old age. Truly, "God protects the Jews."

5. Return from the Netherworld

About the only lasting bit of wisdom I had acquired during my week at the Plinsker yeshivah was that yesterday's food doesn't fill today's stomach. But, while I congratulated myself on having run away while I still had the strength to walk, this did not mean I had turned into a rebel or a free-thinker. What I mean is, in theory I still fully accepted my father's (and everyone else's) assumption that, for a healthy young man who was not conspicuously feebleminded, the only truly worthwhile career was to sit and learn. After all, even at twelve I already understood that a boy who grew up unable to navigate the oceans of the Talmud was, quite simply, not an adult but a large child, a "man of the earth," a half-baked lout destined to be shunned by matchmakers and fit only for the living death of the Czar's army.

So it was not with any great enthusiasm that I packed my total belongings—two shirts and two kerchiefs—and said goodbye to my aunt and uncle.

Aunt Malka had shown me where to get a ticket for the riverboat and had given me two apples and two slices of bread for the voyage; she had cautioned me to eat one apple and one piece of bread no sooner than when the boat reached Vechetsh, and one no later than when we reached Tchervinsk.

Since the whole trip was due to take no more than six hours, I had of course more than enough food. What my aunt, however, had failed to take into account was the fact that it had been an unusually hot summer, and evaporation had left the river so shallow that it required not only a powerful engine but an experienced and alert pilot to keep us from running aground.

About an hour out of Zakhrachin, the deck under our feet began to shudder, and the landscape on both banks abruptly stood still. The pilot cursed, tried to go backwards, fed the boiler till it nearly exploded, but nothing helped. We were firmly stuck in mid-river.

Reading our despair as a rude reflection of his skills, he angrily ordered all passengers to debark onto a narrow, muddy, little sandbank. But even that failed to lighten the boat sufficiently to refloat it.

Huddled on our treeless little desert island, we waited a good few hours in the blazing sun, until a barge, powered by two muscular men with long poles, came by. Noting our predicament, they stopped long enough to have themselves a good laugh, and, as an afterthought, also asked if we needed any help.

This was when we realized that our pilot was the kind of independent character of whom it is said he wouldn't let people help him into his own coffin. In fact, it took nothing less than our threat of open mutiny for him grudgingly to accept one end of a tow-rope. Finally, after enough shouting back and forth to build the Tower of Babel, he got the rope firmly hitched to his front railing, and now ordered his passengers to wade into the mud and get behind the boat and push.

The crewmen of the barge also strained furiously against their poles, and, after a while, to our amazement, the barge actually began to move. However, the only part of our boat that moved with it was the front railing.

At which the bargees, not waiting to listen to our pilot's outraged screams, promptly unhitched their rope, cursed us all roundly to hell, and moved on.

More hours passed, it got to be night, and then morning. Somehow other boats easily managed to avoid our little island and, deaf to our shouts for help (although some of the passengers looked at us as with great interest), navigated the shallow channels on both sides of us without the slightest hesitation. Our pilot swore, pleaded, roared. No one paused long enough even to swear back at him.

By midmorning, when most of us, despite our investment in the ticket, had just about decided to wade ashore and walk back to Zakhrachin, a small steamboat came by, and its captain took pity on us.

In fact, the steamboat's crew even knew where to attach the tow-rope and, in a blessed hour, with various awful scraping noises, and a good deal of shuddering and creaking on the part of both vessels, they hauled us, starving and thirst-tormented, off our barren little island.

But before we'd gone much farther, we realized that *our* boat had sprung a leak and, burdened by the water it had swallowed, it sank by at least another meter, threatening momentarily to swamp the little "engine-room" itself. However, going by the extremely erroneous principle that what is broken already is in no danger of breaking further, we kept forging ahead. Soon we were riding so low in the water we began to scrape bottom again, and the rudder, smothered by the thick, grinding mud, began to drag and soon no longer responded to the pilot at all. This time, though, he did not get too upset because, in the meantime, he had gotten hold of a bottle and managed to let not a drop of it go to waste.

Within minutes, we ran aground once more and, with its leaky bottom and rising cargo of river water, the boat soon began to list like an ocean liner that has been hit by a torpedo.

There was, of course, a happy ending to all this. A modern-looking riverboat turned up and actually stopped. But its captain very sensibly declined to hitch his boat to ours. Instead, after a good deal of mutual recriminations and negotiations, he agreed to rescue the shipwrecked passengers, leaving our lopsided vessel and its stubborn pilot to wait, perhaps for weeks, until the river rose again and either allowed it to proceed or swallowed it up altogether.

I had left Zakhrachin with a fortune of thirty-five kopeks pressed upon me by my aunt and uncle, of which only twenty were needed to pay for my ticket. The balance was, for me, a nice bit of capital, especially since, by my aunt's reckoning, I had been given ample food to last me till Vishogrod.

But, while waiting like a castaway for a boat to rescue us from our sandbank, hunger and thirst and boredom had overwhelmed me, and I had disregarded the scheduling recommended by my aunt. What's more, after eating up the first installment of my provisions, I remembered that devastating moment when, after leaving the yeshivah, I had lost my only piece of bread. So, to guard against another such tragedy, I ate up the remainder of my food as well. Thus, I might now be hungry, but I was rid of anxiety. And, as anyone will tell you, what greater good is there than peace of mind?

In the end, what with all those delays, my six-hour voyage ended up lasting closer to two days. And now that all my food was gone, what did I do on the second day? Well, the Almighty helped and, as they say, there is no misfortune from which *someone* doesn't benefit.

With us on the original boat had been a wedding party, including the groom, all headed for my village, where the wedding was to take place. And since the bride was of poor family, the food and drink for the wedding feast were being furnished by the groom's side. Now here they were, more than twenty hours late for the ceremony, and no village nearby from which one could even send a telegram.

So, on the second day, to console themselves, the heartbroken groom and his relations tapped one of the barrels they had brought along. And since a Jew cannot drink without also having a bite to eat, they soon started on the food as well. As you can imagine, I made sure that I was not overlooked. After all, being a virtual neighbor of the bride, I was, in a sense, the only one representing her side at this premature wedding celebration.

Soon, in fact, I found myself hoping that this boat, too, would run aground, and that we might all remain stranded for as long as the food and drink held out.

And what, you will ask, was happening in Vishogrod during the time when no one knew where I was?

It seemed there had been a tragic little misunderstanding. Every summer, in that portion of the river that connects Plinsk and Zakhrachin, some sort of treacherous undertow claimed the lives of several children. And just the day before, a boy's body had been fished out of the river. Naturally, it was already known that I had run away from the yeshivah and was traveling by way of Zakhrachin, and so our neighbors had helpfully put two and two together and, before anyone had even come forward to identify or claim the body, my parents were informed I was dead.

I am told that my untimely death instantly endowed me in our neighbors' eyes with such labels as "a head like iron," "a young man of pure silk," and a prodigy whose passing impoverished an entire generation. Yet, much as I would have enjoyed hearing these testimonials, I would have given anything for my parents to have been spared such unnecessary grief.

Into the midst of all this excitement, our riverboat arrived. And, since it had obviously been a fairly depressing day for all our neighbors (not to mention the poor, bewildered bride), nearly the whole town gathered at the dock to help the wedding party hastily get settled before candle-lighting time.

Ignored amidst the departing guests, I slunk down the gangplank in the lowest of spirits. Even if I weren't punished, I knew that my return was bound to provoke painful questions about my future. Here I was, already twelve years old, a failure as a scholar, knowing no trade at which I wished to drudge away my life, a burden and embarrassment to family and friends. What would become of me?

As I shuffled almost blindly away from the dock, a woman suddenly let go of a shriek in my ears: "Jews, he's alive! Somebody run and tell his parents."

In an instant, the wedding party was left standing like Lot's wife, and I was half-carried, half-dragged toward my house. I arrived just in time to find my mother on the floor, with neighbors trying to revive her by tugging at her shoulder and screaming into her ear, "Rachel, wake up! He's alive!"

The Rabbi had of course advised my father that until there was positive identification of the body (which, owing to the imminence of *Shabbos* and the dangers of traveling to a Polish village on Saturday night, could not be done before Sunday morning), he need not tear his garment or cover the broken mirror in front of which my mother used to adjust her wig. It was, after all, still only a rumor, and a Jew must live in confidence that the Almighty is a righteous Judge and that restoration of the dead is well within His powers.

But my father, needless to say, lived in a world where rumors might only be rumors, but the bad ones always proved to be true. And so he was even now consulting with the "Holy Fellowship" on my burial arrangements, and a substantial delegation was all prepared to escort my body Sunday morning for such a funeral as would be the envy of the world.

By the time the doctor arrived and gave my mother something to smell from a small bottle and ordered everyone out of the house, it was already almost time to light candles, and my mother suddenly realized she hadn't finished cooking for the Sabbath.

But, as you know, all Jews are responsible for one another, and, within minutes, food began to flow into the house as though we were surrounded by millionaires. While my mother kept protesting it was too much, I, for my part, only wished they would bring more, because all this abundance seemed to me still hopelessly inadequate to appease the appetite I had brought back with me.

Into this tumult, my father arrived home to change his clothes for the Sabbath.

He looked at me with strange eyes and said not one word, but got out his Sabbath boots and began to oil and polish them. His brow darkened still further when he saw all the food that had come pouring in, as though *he* were a beggar, unable to provide for his own family.

Still without a word, he put on his black suit and black hat and left for the synagogue, with not even a glance to see whether I was coming with him. At the time, I wondered, bitterly, if he felt perhaps that a boy who would not study was not in fact better off dead. But today I'm more inclined to believe that my return from the netherworld had so shaken him, he had had to struggle not to burst into tears like a woman and, he may have thought, thereby lose what little authority over me he still had left.

6. A Trade for an Aristocrat

The sensation caused by my return from the dead was not very long-lived, either for me or for my parents, because the food heaped upon us that first Friday afternoon did not (thanks to my rabid appetite) last beyond the Sabbath. And my father's wages as a forester (that is, resident guard, bookkeeper, and supervisor of timbering operations) seemed perfectly suited only to keeping him starving by degrees, instead of all in one gulp.

At that, my father's ten rubles a month were princely wages compared to those of his assistant, the Rabbi's son-in-law. He, on eight rubles, had to feed a wife and six children whom, like my father, he only got to see every other Sabbath. For months, the assistant had been urging my father to go on strike for at least one extra ruble a week. But my father, reared in a wealthy home and perhaps still imbued with a rich man's point of view, argued that there were undoubtedly hundreds of jobless men around who'd be glad to work for even less.

Although I deplored my father's lack of fighting spirit and

ambition, he was of course being perfectly realistic, because once this forest was cut down, it might be years before another job as good as this would turn up. What saved my father, and us, may have been only the fact that he'd been raised to such standards of piety that he was accustomed to fasting every Monday and Thursday. If not for that, he might have died of hunger altogether.

Naturally, during these "seven fat years" there was no way my parents could save money for the lean years inevitably bound to follow. And they arrived a good deal sooner even than expected.

The forest suddenly passed into the hands of new owners, who naturally installed their own trusted men, and, overnight, my father and his fruitful young assistant had to clear out of the little hut deep in the woods, where they had lived each week from Sunday through Friday and, every other week, over the Sabbath as well.

For me, after weeks of total idleness, of fighting with my younger brother Avrohom, of swimming in the river, mountain climbing, and stripping my shirts to play "buttons" with my gentile friends, my father, now brooding about the house like someone who'd been buried the week before, soon became impossible to live with. Truly, for him, idleness was the hardest kind of work.

It had not yet occurred to me that, having closed the door on a life of the mind, I myself was, after all, old enough to look for work to help support the family. In fact, all I dreamt about was leaving home, perhaps even going as far as Warsaw, where my older brother Mordechai now lived; in his infrequent letters he spoke of the responsible position he held in a bakery.

The prospect of spending my days in a large, modern bakery, with its perpetual warmth, its delectable smells, and the unceasing availability of something to eat gripped my imagination and wouldn't let go. Aside from which, if the truth were known, I was sick to death of Vishogrod. During the few short weeks I'd been away, the whole town seemed to have changed. Not one of my

friends was left. Those who were too dumb or too rebellious to go
on to yeshivah had been apprenticed to various trades, and some
had even been sent to other towns in quest of work or training.
Only I remained, nearly thirteen, and doing nothing with my life.
The situation was intolerable, not only to my parents, but now,
with my father constantly about the house, to me as well.

The question was, what to do in a small town like Vishogrod
with a boy of working age, who clearly lacked the stamina or brains
for a scholarly life?

If anyone had troubled to ask me, I would have told them I
was more than ready to go and join Mordechai in Warsaw, which
I pictured as a vast modern metropolis glittering with golden
opportunities for making money, the frantic pursuit of exquisite
pleasures, and altogether a degree of modish living we villagers
dared not dwell on even in our thoughts, for fear of violating the
commandment, "Thou shalt not covet."

But my father, while in principle he had nothing against
Warsaw, held to the belief that a boy's only assurance of seizing
his golden opportunity in life lay in having a skilled craft in his
hand before he left home. "A skill is a kingdom," he would say,
in a play on the words *m'lokho* and *m'lukho*. And I quite understood his concern. Having sunk so low after a childhood of fairy-
tale luxury and a wedding contract guaranteeing him "sustenance
in perpetuity," he was determined that *his* sons' security would
rest upon no man's promises, but, aside from our Father in heaven,
depend solely on the work of their own hands. While he had
nothing against the baker's trade, he didn't feel I was mature
enough to be trusted out of his sight.

For a brief while, I had a reprieve. Winter was over, the snow
had melted, and we children could once more get out of our dark,
narrow homes and go running barefoot in the streets. Now began
a brief season when even the poorest boys and girls could make
some money. It was the time of baking matzos for Passover, and
there was work for everyone, regardless of age.

But right after Passover, my parents took up the question

anew. High schools and universities of course being as unattainable as the moon to a Jew without money or *protektzia*, what was to become of a big, strapping lout like me? Once again it was impressed upon me that, of my contemporaries, this one already had been apprenticed to a tailor, that one to a shoemaker, while a third was still in yeshivah and, unlike myself, one day would surely astonish the world with the razorlike subtlety of his insights.

What did I want to do—wait till I was old enough to be conscripted into Fonya's army, where, with my sadly deficient Jewish education, there was nothing to preserve me from being turned into a bloodthirsty Russianized oaf, if not actually into a Christian?

Call me spoiled, if you will, but none of the trades being learned by my friends exactly made my mouth water. So, in consideration of my high-class family origins, it was finally decided to prepare me for a more "aristocratic" career. My father made a deal with Leibke the watchmaker, and early one morning he took me by the hand and led me over to Leibke's shop, hard by the pig market.

After all, said my father as he consoled me with one of his rare smiles, a watchmaker is also a professional, almost a doctor of sorts, although not enjoying the same profitable partnership with the Angel of Death.

If one look at the outside of the place was enough to make my heart fall out, this was nothing compared to the shock of meeting Leibke himself. The watchmaker was a wisp of a man, almost a midget, but what he lacked in overall stature he made up for by the size of his head, which was decorated with a pair of mad red eyes in a creased little face divided by a nose curved like a Turkish scimitar.

Leibke's house consisted of two parts. The front section, which had a window, was the store. The half without the window was where he and his family made their home. I took a stealthy glimpse into that eternal darkness, and found its furnishings made up of two foolish beds whose straw never ceased to leak out of the mattresses and, combined with the dried mud, covered the floor like a carpet.

I think most children are raised to expect that a bed stands on four legs. But Leibke's beds rested confidently on such casual makeshifts as a stack of bricks, a chunk of firewood, and a vinegar jar.

There was one other piece of conspicuous furniture, a foul-smelling tub, of which more in a moment. But if Leibke lacked worldly possessions, he was more than generously blessed with children.

I tried to count how many, but the moment one ran out, two others came in, then three went out, and finally the only one who stayed in the same place long enough to let itself be counted was the baby, whom the tub served as a cradle, and who was at this moment screaming for help as if someone had poured boiling water on it.

In the store, my father was still waiting for Leibke to lift his head and acknowledge his presence. But the watchmaker was concentrating, one eye closed entirely, the other surrounded by a wooden ring with glass in it, through which he was peering madly deep into the bowels of a dismantled watch.

I was, for the moment, rather impressed by any trade that made it possible for a man to ignore my father. But in due course Leibke raised his head, deigned to recognize his visitor, and even affected to remember their agreement. Thus I found out for the first time that I already belonged to Leibke for the next six years.

Looking me over, for which he had to stand on tiptoe, Leibke made it sound as though he weren't quite sure what had made him bestow such a kindness upon me, and I was desperately hoping for him to say that he had changed his mind.

Instead, just in case I had dreamt I would begin to learn about watches at once, Leibke now made clear to me that, for the first two years, my duty was to do nothing but obey him and his wife. This meant doing whatever household chores they required, such as carrying water, emptying the slop pails, sweeping the floors and, above all, rocking and carrying the baby.

I was so stunned by this, I forgot my manners enough to ask, "Do I have to nurse the baby, too?"

At this, Leibke sprang to his feet, pointed a finger at my nose, and screamed, *"Sheigatz!* I'll teach you to open a mouth when the master speaks!"

So it seemed that this little man, hardly bigger than a matchstick, was already my "master"! I stood there, boiling inside, staring down at Leibke, who was less than half my size, and if my father hadn't still been in the room, I might have said a word or two on how I felt about this whole transaction.

As it was, I had to look on in silence while Leibke handed my father a scrap of paper, and my father obediently signed it, then turned to me with a sigh and, as though asking my forgiveness, pointed out once more that I was, after all, learning an "aristocratic" trade.

It was settled that I would start on the new moon, nine days from then. As I left, holding tightly to my father's hand, all I could think of was how to keep from falling into the clutches of that angry little man.

But the nine days were over before I knew it, and early one morning I started my apprenticeship, going with all the appetite of a conscript on his way to serve the Czar, and thinking bitterly how a proud man like my father had humbled himself, and enslaved me, only because he no longer felt like a man.

When I arrived, the master was still in *shul,* but his wife was already up and about. I judged her to be a fairly young woman, whose hard life had already turned her into a dusty, shriveled hag.

But any pity I might have felt for her quickly vanished when she turned on me, afraid I might stand idle for a moment, and, in a pause between her baby's unheeded shrieks, demanded to know how many invitations I needed to pour out the slops. Following this aristocratic task, she showed me how to sweep the floor with her crippled broom. It seemed no use telling her that all this accomplished was to stir up the mud beneath the straw.

Finally the master came home, unburdened of his angry prayers, and, seeing I was finished with the broom and had found nothing else to do, he swooped down on me with a shout of rage. "*Yungatch!* What are you standing there like a *golem?* Don't you hear the child crying?"

I approached the cradle, terrified. Below me, in the tub, I saw a shrunken little demon screaming curses up at the heavens. With palsied hands, I tried to rock the tub without tipping it over. But the creature inside had already taken a poisonous dislike to me and, for spite, cried even louder. During this, the little master stood watching me with his red, ferocious eyes as though it were all my fault.

Out in the street, I could hear boys not much younger than I playing ball, or hitching rides on passing wagons, while I, overnight, had been transformed into a servant girl.

Meanwhile the baby didn't stop shrieking, and its mother finally bestirred herself. Not, heaven forbid, to pick up her misfortune with her own hands. No. She sprang up with a mouthful of curses at her little husband and demanded, "Why aren't you sending the apprentice out with the child?"

The master obeyed at once. He wrapped it up in the nearest rag and handed me the package. "Go take it out."

I asked, "Where should I take it?"

At this, he became enraged, and passed on to me all the curses he had absorbed from his wife, with a few of his own thrown in. He also accused me of pretending to be even more stupid than I was, and taking advantage of his patience because it was my first day on the job. But just wait until tomorrow!

I took the screaming bundle and fled.

Outside, all the rest of the morning, I trudged up and down the sweet, mud-paved streets, holding the little demon like some carrier of a contagious disease.

Choked with envy, I watched boys no younger than myself at games my state of servitude would never allow me to play again, and could have sunk into the ground when I looked up and found them pointing and grinning at me and the thing in my arms.

Then the baby did something I would rather not describe, and my first impulse was to drop it in the nearest gutter, wash my hands at the pump and, as I was, flee into the world, an outcast and a wanderer like Cain.

I compromised by running back to Leibke's house, ducking in the back way, gently dumping his little treasure back into its foul trough, and escaping unseen.

But, while I walked the streets now, wondering if there was any point in my ever going home again, Leibke must have heard or smelled what I had faithfully returned to him. He tore off his apron and trotted directly over to my father with the scream of one who had been looted by the Cossacks. "Your renegade of a son! He ran away from the job. He's broken our agreement!"

I am told that, at first, my father was furious at me. But then, as Leibke continued to insult him, virtually in front of half the town, my father took the agreement Leibke was waving in his face, and, without much ceremony, tore it in half. Then he seized the little watchmaker by the collar and pitched him out.

Meanwhile, in despair, I had gone to my Aunt Tzivia's house and told her I was running off to Warsaw, with or without a pass from the police. While she was still trying to calm me, my mother arrived, told me what had happened, and reported that my father said to come home—I would not have to continue my apprenticeship.

I returned like a man reprieved from the firing squad, which is not an idle turn of phrase because, half a dozen years later, as you will see before long, I had occasion to experience that pleasure as well.

The way it turned out, my father, who, for all his strictness, also knew when to let a child have his own way, had already inquired at the magistrate's. If I was still determined to go to Warsaw, I could have a travel permit within three days.

For a moment I felt the full terror of leaving home for the second and possibly last time. But, even at thirteen, the great world drew me like a magnet, and I knew that if I stayed I would only have to submit to another apprenticeship.

My father, as somber as the day he would see me off to war, took my hand and went with me to the magistrate. And never before or since did I love him so desperately as on that day.

7. A Cosmopolitan Way of Life

To me, the memorable thing about being thirteen was not my bar mitzvah, a celebration disposed of on a Monday morning with no more fanfare than putting on a fresh, still-creaking pair of *tefillin* and tasting my first glass of brandy. It was the fact that my father finally agreed there was no future for me in our town, and allowed me to depart for Warsaw and lead my own life.

Tuesday was when Tuviah the teamster carried goods and passengers to Warsaw. I'd already received my police permit to travel, and could hardly wait to escape our village and its backward ways, and begin to share my brother Mordechai's liberated and cosmopolitan way of life.

My brief experience in Vishogrod as a matzo baker already had convinced me that I could work the same hours and at the same speed as a grown man, and Mordechai, in his letters, had assured me that he could get me a job like his, as a baker's assistant, which seemed to me a very adult and responsible profession.

It was a bitterly cold spring day and my mother, who had insisted on traveling with me, pounded·her feet and shivered beside me on Tuviah's crude open wagon. Harnessed to this vehicle were two moribund horses, who clearly had been better trained in how to fast than how to run. Friends and relatives had come to see us off, and piously wished us that we might arrive in Warsaw without the loss of any fingers or toes to frostbite, as sometimes happened to people who rode with Tuviah, a man who attracted small disasters the way bare feet attract splinters.

Unlike my mother, I felt no discomfort whatever. Tall and proud as a general, I sat beside her on a crate of eggs, one foot resting on a live calf and the other dangling jauntily over the side. Imagine, I thought, here I am traveling to Warsaw, a place where people eat white bread in the middle of the week, and you drink hot tea with lemon and sugar even when you're healthy.

But just as we started to leave town, it occurred to me that if I was truly going to make a career for myself in the great world, now was as good a time as any to begin standing on my own feet. I persuaded my mother to go back home, and Tuviah obligingly stopped his horses, although you would have needed a microscope to distinguish between their walking and their standing still. Before climbing down, my mother handed me my baggage, all of it tied up in one red kerchief, a chunk of bread with an onion, and, although I was on my way to a liberated new life, my prayerbook and *tefillin*.

Then she said goodbye to me with as many tears as it would have taken to dispatch one's son to fight the Turk. I, for my part, wasn't laughing either. But I comforted myself with the thought that, big as Warsaw was, I wouldn't let it gulp me down.

As an afterthought, my mother gave me Mordechai's address. She didn't know where he worked, but after all I could wait for him in his room.

In the next few hours the wagon passed through various other villages and began to fill up with passengers. One of them was Laizer, a leather dealer who, being a Hasid, did not permit himself to sit next to a strange woman. And so, before I knew it, a healthy pair of hands had lifted me and put me down as a buffer between himself and Guta Yerel, the midwife.

At first I was insulted at being handled like a child. But, since Guta weighed at least 250 pounds, I soon saw the benefit of being sandwiched between two such warm, well-padded bodies. To add to my comfort, a drunken Pole sat directly behind me, and soon dozed off and started to wheeze like a sick horse. The alcoholic fumes he exhaled began to warm the back of my neck, and when they reached my nose I became pleasantly drowsy, and slumped against the fat midwife as though she were a pile of soft feather bedding.

I was awakened by a scream of outrage. All around me was darkness as deep as the ninth plague. What had happened? While riding through the Rysovar forest, that historic den of highway-men and horse-thieves which the Polish police avoided like the evil eye, something very simple had occurred. With the passengers huddled for warmth into a tight, slumbering knot, and Tuviah up front, surrounded by a curtain of snow, sleeping as sweetly as any paying passenger, someone had quietly walked alongside and un-harnessed the better of the two horses. His accomplices had helped push the wagon so that it never slowed until the stolen horse was far away.

Tuviah first noticed something was wrong when the wagon began to stutter to a crawl. Half in his sleep, he shouted the Polish equivalent of "giddap," and automatically brought his whip down on the healthier horse.

When he realized he was beating the air, he woke up al-together, saw what they had done to him, and for a moment alternated between cursing the thieves and beating the innocent horse they had left him.

His passengers, too, now came to life, encouraging Tuviah with cries of, "What are you waiting for?" and "Let's catch them!"

But no one made a move except the unfortunate Tuviah

himself, who jumped down and began to circle the wagon, and even looked underneath, as though his good horse merely might have gotten mislaid.

In the end, of course, everyone had to get off and help push, while Tuviah walked in front, bitterly leading the horse even the thieves didn't want.

On the icy road, sometimes the horse fell, sometimes Tuviah did, and sometimes both of them together. Since no one had taken any notice of me, I stayed on the wagon and tried to go back to sleep. But I missed the warmth and comfort of being squeezed between Laizer and Guta Yerel, both of whom were huffing and pushing behind me.

At daybreak, the exhausted passengers cheered up a little. A town was visible in the distance. With a renewed burst of strength, horse and wagon were dragged and pushed until we reached the inn.

Here, no one seemed the least bit surprised at our calamity, and the good news of our arrival spread like the rumors preceding a holy man. A number of Polish peasants soon arrived with horses for sale. To their credit, be it said that not one of them tried to sell us back our own horse.

In the taproom of the inn, meanwhile, the men among the passengers, not counting the Pole, lost no time taking out *tallis* and *tefillin*, and even the women brought out their womanish prayerbooks, and, possibly to help us keep warm, we said our prayers with such fervor, a cloud of steam soon hovered over our heads.

Afterwards, we all, myself included, moved up to the counter and, after a few glasses of vodka, felt a good deal more cheerful about continuing our journey.

First, of course, we all had to have a bite. Only I realized that, after splurging on two glasses of schnapps, I could no longer afford a piece of bread and herring. I still had money in my pocket but, even though a glass of hot tea with sugar was only a kopek, my total capital was limited to the equivalent of maybe sixty cents, which had to last me until I got a job.

Back in the wagon, where I made sure of getting my old seat between Guta Yerel and the chaste leather dealer, a new comedy now developed. The horse Tuviah had hired to pull us into Warsaw was strong and well rested, while the old one, which he had inherited from his father, liked every so often to stand in one spot and admire the scenery.

As a result, when Tuviah cracked his whip, the new horse eagerly lurched forward. But, held back by its partner, it ended up with its front legs doing a futile little dance in the air, while the old horse remained nailed to the spot, dreaming its horsy dreams. Tuviah unleashed a string of deadly oaths along with his whip. But his tired old horse merely turned around with a look of reproach, as though wondering whether Tuviah could possibly mean *him*.

Bystanders soon gathered and started favoring us with the usual sort of good advice. One peasant said we should have the horse change places with the passengers. Another suggested we hang a bundle of straw under his nose and set fire to it, and the other recommendations were all on a similar high level.

The end result was that Tuviah had to hire another fresh horse. He declared bitterly that, after the years he'd spent training his horse to go without food, the innkeeper had spoiled it by feeding it too much.

We had been due to arrive in Warsaw at noon. We got there shortly before midnight. Almost at once, I saw some of the wonders I'd heard about: cobbled streets free of mud, horseless trams running on tracks, buildings so tall you wondered what kept them from tumbling over like a house of cards, and, funniest of all, men wearing short coats and stiff collars.

The fortune of sixty kopeks I clutched in my pocket spared me the need to look for a hotel. However, since it was still a long time to sunrise, I thought I might as well look for a place to sleep.

My nose led me to a stable filled with hay. I crawled in, covered myself, and didn't wake up again until, what seemed like minutes later, a large hand, reaching in for a load of hay, pulled one of my feet out with it.

Since it was now broad daylight, I began walking the streets, asking people how to get to my brother's address. After several hours of being spun like a *dreidel* in all four directions, I found the street and number. My brother's lodgings turned out to be on the fifth floor of a four-story house. I climbed up to the attic and knocked. A shriveled old woman in a robe which seemed to have been stitched together out of dishrags opened the door, peered at me blindly, went back to find her glasses, and then demanded to know what the devil I wanted.

I told her I was the brother of Mordechai the baker.

The name seemed to mean absolutely nothing to her. With a sinking heart, I insisted that this was the address I'd been given. After some further evasion, she finally allowed that some baker boys were living there, and if my brother was one of them, he came home to sleep only on Friday nights.

It seemed to me very strange that my brother should need to sleep only one night a week. Meanwhile, I had a glimpse of what she meant by home. It was a narrow room with a diagonal wall and no ceiling whatever. Under this wall was crammed a row of narrow beds, each of them covered with straw-filled sacks and pillows.

I stood and thought what to do. The old woman either didn't know or wouldn't tell where my brother was working, and here it was only Wednesday. What to do with myself till Friday? Since I'd indulged myself in a breakfast of coffee and a roll, I had only about fifty-seven kopeks left to my name, and nowhere to sleep. Yet my feelings in that wretched place were such that I couldn't get myself to ask the old woman if I could use Mordechai's bed until he turned up.

So I spent the day prowling the wondrous wide streets of Warsaw, marveling over a hundred things I had never seen before.

Finally, I stopped in front of a little café which I'd been told by a shopkeeper served as an office for several small employment agents.

As soon as I approached the place, two ragged little men in bowler hats with canes in their hands came running out and fell upon me like hungry cats cornering a fat mouse.

Each man pulled out his little notebook and took my name. I admitted that I had no address, and therefore wasn't yet registered with the police, but they seemed willing to overlook that. I was happy to see unemployed boys of thirteen were so much in demand, after all. But now, both men put out their hands and stared at me. I stared back, bewildered. Finally, one of them hissed, "Advance on commission. One ruble."

I told them I didn't have a ruble, but as soon as they found me a job. . . .

Both fiercely crossed out my name in their books and told me to go to the devil back where I came from.

This brought to mind that, even if I'd wanted to go home, I didn't have the return fare. Night was falling once again, and I had been told that if the police caught me without a legal place of residence, I would wish I had never seen Warsaw.

Meanwhile, inside the café sat boys with their mothers, boys with their fathers, candidates for high school, all being urged to eat up, not showing as much as a moment's embarrassment at the envious way I sat on a bench outside and watched them. Finally, one mother feeding a runny-nosed boy was sensitive enough to come out and beg me to stop staring, because I was spoiling her son's appetite.

I moved my seat and tried to look elsewhere. Business began to thin out. It was dark now, but I was more troubled by the growling of my stomach than by thoughts of the police. I started up a hopeful conversation with a waiter who looked faintly familiar. He turned out to be a *landsman* from Vishogrod!

He asked me if I didn't have relatives in Warsaw. Did I have relatives! I had a brother, a baker. What more did I need? He dismissed my brother with a wave of his hand. A baker, he said, is no longer a human being.

But he's still my brother!

A boy who works as a baker, he patiently explained, is already half-dead. His very life no longer belongs to him. What is the good of a brother like that?

His words left a chill around my heart. I now understood why my brother slept in his room only on Friday nights. The rest of the week he didn't have enough time to go home.

The waiter saw how depressed his words had left me. He took me into the kitchen and found me something to eat.

By the time I'd finished eating it was midnight once again. The restaurant closed, the waiters were swallowed up by the darkness, and I still had no place to sleep. My *landsman* also had warned me that any homeless boy found in the streets at night first is given a warm welcome in the cellars of the police station, and then is deported back to where he came from, which at the moment seemed to me even more terrible than what they might do to me in jail.

Cautiously, I made my way back to my brother's lodgings, felt my way up five flights in total darkness, and banged on the door. No one answered. After a while, I stopped banging and fell asleep in front of the door.

Before long, though, I was awakened by the janitor who'd heard me sneaking up the stairs. He was holding a lit candle so close to my face I could feel it singe my eyebrows.

Brother or no brother, he warned me that if he ever again caught me sleeping on the stairs, he'd turn me in to the police.

I went back down into the freezing street. Every bone ached. I couldn't stop yawning. I tried to tell myself not to lose courage. Then I quickly searched my pockets to make sure the janitor hadn't robbed me. Thank heaven, my wealth was intact.

Unseen, I plodded the dark streets to keep my toes from freezing, and after some hours the sun grudgingly rose.

I now began in earnest to look for a job of any kind, simply to tide me over till Friday afternoon. But before the day was over, I realized there were literally hundreds of boys like myself, all freshly arrived from the provinces, unregistered by the police, also looking for any kind of job.

While I was standing with a group of these boys, wondering whether I wouldn't do better alone, a middle-aged couple arrived, looked us over like cattle dealers on market day, and decided on me.

"Want a job?"

"What kind?" I said stupidly.

"You want or you don't want?"

By now it was as cold as it was dark, and where was I going to spend the night? I said, "I'll take it."

They had me follow them home, where they put a plate of bread and herring with tea in front of me. ("Balanced menus," you must understand, are entirely an American invention. In my day, before growers and manufacturers had learned to steal the vitamins out of our food, people were able to live and thrive on a diet of little more than bread, raw onions, cabbage, tea, herring, and boiled kasha, and maybe some fresh fruit in the summer. Even today, I still think of green salads as grass for the cows.) I ate silently, still afraid to ask what they expected of me. Then I waited to be shown my room. The master nodded for me to follow him down a flight of groaning wooden steps. The cellar contained a barrel of dirty water and what looked like a thousand empty, mud-caked beer bottles. I looked at him.

"Get to work," he said, not unkindly.

I was to wash each one, inside and out, before going to sleep. What choice did I have? The boss watched as I set to work, and complimented me on my energy and neatness. Then he proceeded to tap a barrel and fill the bottles I had washed.

In this manner, it got to be one o'clock, two o'clock, three o'clock, and I was still washing bottles. My fingers were stiff with cold, and since my boss was working as though it were broad daylight, I felt embarrassed to ask him when his workers were expected to sleep.

I'd already given up looking at the time, when the boss's wife suddenly shouted down, "Let him go to sleep already, or he'll run off like the others."

The boss nodded like a man who has learned to be tolerant of human weakness. He pulled out a sack filled with straw, and smoothed it down against the floor. "You can sleep now, if you like," he said like a man who understood that a child cannot be expected to work like a man.

Although I didn't care for his tone, I fell onto the straw mattress as though from a great height, and think I was asleep before I even closed my eyes. But I'd barely had time to turn over, when I found the boss's wife tugging impatiently at my shoulder. Half-asleep, with darkness still covering the windows as thickly as it covered my eyes, I was back washing bottles.

During the day I was sent with a sack from tavern to tavern to collect more empty bottles, and my bosses kept me so busy with that, I never even had the chance to ask about food.

By evening, I was staggering like a drunk, and quite willing to forget about supper if they would just let me sleep for a while. But the boss again gave me some bread and herring and, as kindly as ever, explained that on Thursday nights all the bottles had to be filled for Saturday night deliveries. Therefore, just that once, it was customary to work all night. But to make up for this, he would let me sleep all Friday night and all day Saturday.

He made it sound as though only a monster of ingratitude would fail to see how reasonable his request was. But I had simply gone too long without sleep. And since, in the last two days, I had earned the equivalent of exactly seventeen kopeks, and tomorrow I was sure to see my brother, I decided I could afford to be independent. When I told him he could keep his job, the boss was almost speechless with indignation. Never in this world had he encountered such impertinence. A boy who expected to eat without working! He had no doubt that, with luck, I would end up before a firing squad. (About which, as I mentioned already, he wasn't too far wrong. But that's another story.) He also declined to pay me my wages.

Once more, my problem was how to get through the night without being arrested. On Nalevka street I met another homeless boy, and he took me to his quarters, an abandoned bakery, where I had my first good night's sleep since I had left home.

In the morning I awoke full of happy anticipation. At last it was Friday. Today I would see my brother, and he'd see to it that I had a job and a place to lay my head. It was agony to wait until evening.

Toward sunset, I stationed myself in front of the house where my brother had his bed. I didn't know whether he would come directly home, or go to the synagogue first. But I wanted to take no chances of missing him.

It was getting dark already, when I noticed two ragged human skeletons dragging themselves along the pavement. They moved on scrawny, tottering legs and seemed, every so often, barely to be able to keep one another from pitching face down into the mud, they were so paralyzed with sleep. It took me some time to recognize one of these ghosts as my brother. I ran to throw my arms around him. He gave me a blank look and went right on past me.

I cried, "Mordechai, it's me, your brother Jacob." But he and his companion kept on, as though afraid to lose their momentum. They staggered up the stairs like a pair of drunks on an icy road. I followed close behind them, ready to catch Mordechai when he fell. But he somehow made it up to the attic floor and lurched into his dormitory. Before he could lie down, I grabbed his arm and once again tried to remind him who I was.

He peered at me with eyes no longer able to focus. Finally, by way of a *sholom aleichem*, he extended a limp hand covered with flour and dough, then told his landlady, "Give him to eat," and fell on his bed as though he'd been shot.

To tell the truth, I was beginning to feel a little unwelcome.

Here it was *Shabbos,* the one day in the week on which it is forbidden to fast, and while tonight I might have inherited Mordechai's portion, I surely couldn't also expect to eat for him tomorrow. At the same time, if I had any notion of being allowed to use one of the beds, it was only minutes before each one of them was filled with a bakery boy, all in roughly the same condition as my brother. Their snores, which weren't long in coming, began to sound like a railroad station where several trains were getting up steam. It was a terrifying sight.

The landlady tugged at my arm and pointed to a little bench on which she had put down some food for me. But either the snores, or the food itself, had killed my appetite. The moment her back was turned I started to lie down on the floor next to my brother's bed, and a thick cloud of sleep smothered me almost at once. Yet my final waking thoughts were of utter contentment. I felt at peace. I had, after all, known from the first that as soon as I found my brother he would take care of me.

8. The Smell of Fresh Bread

For boys like me, who at age thirteen or fourteen had come to Warsaw to make their fortunes, the authorities had a foolproof system. You couldn't get a job unless you had a place to live, and no landlady could rent you so much as a straw mattress unless you had a job.

Somehow, my brother Mordechai, in his harassed, infrequent letters, had forgotten to mention this, too. However, true to his word, the moment the Sabbath was over, he took me back with him to his bakery and saw to it that I got a job, permit or no permit.

By the time the night was over, I'd already begun to get a picture of what it meant, back in those simple, unspoiled days, to be a baker's apprentice. And then I understood why, even among boys as hungry and homeless as myself, the kind of person who voluntarily became a baker was believed to be someone whom even his parents no longer expected to grow up into a human being. Such a boy, after he'd already been thrown out of the house, which I think you know a Jewish family doesn't do lightly, was often apt to end up sleeping on top of the oven in a bakery, which in my day was an almost traditional place of refuge. Then, after he had hung around the bakery for some time and kept his eyes open, as soon as one of the other employees, almost inevitably, collapsed of fatigue or caught pneumonia, he was in a perfect strategic position to inherit the job.

That, however, was not the way it had happened to Mordechai. He had come to Warsaw innocently, ready to take any kind of honest work and, after hungering for several days, simply had been attracted in passing by the smell of fresh bread.

Almost at the moment he had set foot in the store, half-hypnotized by the intoxicating odors, he had found himself signed up for an apprenticeship of three years, for a salary of ten rubles a year, plus meals and sleeping privileges on the bake-oven. (And if that sounds to you like good money, remember that my father managed to starve very nicely on ten rubles a *month.*)

The word "union," of course, was unheard of, and a good working day could sometimes run for twenty-two or even twenty-four hours. To make up for this, however, you were free all Friday night and all day *Shabbos* until sundown. The moment after *havdoloh,* though, the boys panted back to the bakery like condemned souls being lashed by demons and didn't see sunlight again till—with luck—the end of the week.

Unlike New York (whose bakeries, several decades earlier, already had steam-driven machinery even for matzo baking), all the kneading, mixing, and baking in Warsaw at the turn of the century still was done by hand. In addition, wood had to be chopped for the ovens, barrels of water hauled from the well, and flour from 200-pound sacks dumped into huge vats and kneaded by hand.

I remember the shock it gave me the first time I saw my brother and two other boys immersed and struggling through one of these swamps of flour and water, while the sweat ran freely off their brows and arms into the dough, and one of them, if you'll forgive my mentioning it, had a runny nose adding its steady drip to the mixture.

Thus they stood day after day, night after night, asleep on their feet while their hands continued to push, to stir, to clench and unclench. Already by Monday they truly no longer knew when it was day and when it was night.

Except when things were busy, they got a breather for two or three hours shortly before dawn. During that time they didn't know what to do first—wash, eat, sleep, or say their morning prayers.

Frequently, a boy would put on his *tefillin* and fall asleep. But almost before he could start to snore, he was awakened and chased back to work.

The quality of the baked goods produced under such conditions I leave to your imagination. It would happen sometimes that customers returned loaves of bread in which various unexpected articles had been found—a penknife, some eggshells, a cuff torn from a shirt, or, most frequently of all, a half-smoked cigarette.

In such cases, the offending bread was cheerfully exchanged for another, and that was the end of it.

Only once did it happen that a woman came running in with a cry of outrage, and there were so many other women with her, they blocked the street. What had she found in the bread that was so terrible? The housing of the *tefillin* which are worn on the head. Obviously, one of the bakers had fallen asleep while praying, and when awakened and sent back to work, he had tried to finish his prayers while standing over the vat. Apparently he had dozed off once more, and none of the other bakers were sufficiently awake to notice that his head *tefillin* had fallen into the dough.

A perfectly understandable accident, I would have thought. But this woman insisted that the offending baker should be arrested and deported back to his home town, no less.

The master finally managed to calm her down by pointing out that this particular man happened to be the cleanest worker they had, because at least he didn't smoke. The offending worker, for his part, was less concerned about losing his job than he was about finding out whether his *tefillin*, after having been baked, still were fit to be used.

The following week, when my brother told me of a slightly better job available at another bakery, I thanked him kindly and decided to pass it up. In fact, hungry as I usually was, it took some time before I could once again sink my teeth heartily into a chunk of fresh bread.

9. The Great Warsaw Labor Dispute

During the seven, eight years I worked in Warsaw, not one of my jobs had any kind of future in it. They were simply a way to keep alive, and sometimes barely that. But, as they say, "if you work to eat and eat to work, where's the profit?"

My sympathies, as I rolled from one place of exploitation to another, were of course totally with those inept, idealistic souls who, like myself, entertained vague and feverish dreams of revolution while meekly remaining enslaved to a job which, at best, kept us on our feet no less than eighteen to twenty hours a day.

You will ask, how did a boy of my intelligence and energy in all that time not manage to learn a skilled trade—except, as it turned out, that of labor agitator, which was neither very skilled nor much of a trade? But in my day, being an apprentice with a signed contract meant your time and work belonged totally to a master who, for the first two years, was under no obligation to teach you anything at all.

Besides, it seemed to me futile to plan for the future when, at age twenty-one, I was dead certain to become what my father, with bitter understatement, called "the Czar's *eidem oyf kest*" (kept son-in-law) for a period of service during which I'd be lucky merely to remember I was a Jew.

And so, although my young blood craved excitement, I merely drifted from one deadening job to another. Aside from revolution, which I personally felt in no position to start, what *were* the possibilities for excitement? On what I earned there was certainly not much use in looking for a girl with whom to keep serious company. And I had not yet, thank Heaven, become dehumanized enough to seek out the other kind. (As my uncle would have said, "How many sins already are worth all the trouble it takes to perform them?")

Much of the credit for preserving my virtue of course must be shared with my various masters who, if it were possible, would have worked me twenty-five hours a day, nine days a week. Thus, over the years, my youthful revolutionary passion gradually became less universal and began to focus instead on our immediate exploiters, most of whom themselves were only a few inches away from starvation.

At this time, the business of organizing workers, negotiating with bosses and, if necessary, calling strikes, was something none of us knew, as they say, with which fork to pick up. To give you some idea of what it was that finally made us desperate enough to call the first general labor walkout ever seen in Warsaw, let me give you the pleasure of meeting some of the capitalists for whom I worked during those long, lean years. I will name no names, so as not to shame any descendants or relatives they might have in America.

Today, in Columbus's country, I know it's customary to grumble about how the unions are growing too big, too powerful, too arrogant. I don't deny that, in the benign American climate, some of them might have, as it says in the Scriptures, "waxed fat." But don't forget what conditions were like before there were unions, especially back in Warsaw, when even to talk about organizing labor made you a candidate for the unwelcome attention of the police and its wretched, underpaid spies.

We were, in short, completely at the mercy of our masters, some of whom were decent (and sometimes paid for it by going bankrupt), but many of whom seemed no longer able to remember that their workers were defenseless Jewish children and not dogs.

To begin with, after seeing how my brother Mordechai was enslaved, I had lost all desire for him to use his influence on my behalf. What I fancied instead was a job in a clean place like a grocery store. Jobs like that were naturally not just waiting for a strange boy to walk in and ask for. However, after prowling the streets for several days without a place to eat or to lay my head, I hit it lucky.

It was a small, well-kept wholesale food store, and my wages were to be five rubles per semester, plus food but not sleeping quarters. Still, God helped, and my new boss left me so little time to sleep, I hardly noticed the lack of a bed.

I plunged into the job with great joy. The first morning I was presented with a sack containing 144 pounds of sugar. It was to be delivered to a store five blocks away. I didn't walk but almost danced all the way, dreaming of the day, six months from then, when five rubles would be counted out on the table for me. I had already figured out that I would send two rubles to my parents, save one for emergencies, and with the remaining two would outfit myself from head to toe.

When I made my delivery, the storekeeper seemed so impressed with my enthusiasm that he tipped me two kopeks. With these I bought two rolls and returned, empty-handed, taking a step and a bite, a bite and a step, and at this moment wouldn't have changed places with Rothschild himself.

In the evening, my new master locked up the warehouse, and everyone went home to sleep. Everyone except me. Until I got paid, six months from then, I hadn't the money even to rent space on a straw mattress in some crowded attic.

So I dragged myself around the streets in pouring rain, feeling each door shut tightly against me, and hiding like a thief from every police patrol, because I had already been in Warsaw for two weeks and still hadn't registered myself and my place of residence.

The steam rose from my clothes as from an oven, and as for my boots, at least one of them was up to the occasion. That is, it had a hole in front and a hole in the side, which allowed the water running in at one end a convenient way of running out again. This only goes to prove that the Almighty never sends a plague without also sending the remedy.

Finally, at the edge of town, I found an empty shed with a roof, where I slept that night and for many nights to come.

Actually, in my "clean" job I was not much better off than a baker. I, too, worked eighteen to twenty hours a day, and before *yom tov* a full twenty-four. For workers in my position the only salvation was *Shabbos*. Without that one day of rest, none of us could have survived. And yet, it was part of the new revolutionary doctrine that such concessions to religious superstition had to be abolished.

What the bosses didn't realize was that decent hours and wages would have benefited them as much as us. You know the saying, "Treat a broomstick like a human being, it will act like a human being." But a boy who worked eighteen hours a day was usually in such a stupor he could make the most elementary mistakes. Once a baker came running to my boss, screaming that instead of twenty pounds of sugar, I'd delivered twenty pounds of salt, which his boys promptly had kneaded into the dough, ruining his entire output of *challah* for that *Shabbos*.

My boss, faced with a demand for full compensation, calmly pointed out that the mistake could not have been made by me, who got at least two to three hours of sleep every night, but by the baker's own employees, who got no sleep at all between Thursday and Friday.

Things were no better for boys who had apprenticed themselves to tailors, shoemakers, or in other trades. Nor, on the other hand, could I claim that our employers licked honey as a result of the exploitation of their workers. About our neighbor, Yossel the shoemaker, they used to say he had so many debts that even his hair didn't belong to him. Moishe the tailor on our street lived in a one-room shack together with a wife, three grown daughters, two infants, and four assistants at full room and board. On cold nights the cow was also brought into the house. Heaven only knows where all twelve of them found room to lie down. The only benefit he had was that the apprentices had virtually no choice but to marry the daughters and then, on borrowed or secretly saved-up money, move out to usually less-elegant places of their own.

That was how we and our dear ones lived for generations. Yet they were healthier than the people I see around me in America today, may they live and be well. Perhaps because they didn't overeat. But, it must be admitted, they also went about marked by looks of perpetual anxiety. Nothing ever came easy to them, and the smallest disaster could wipe them out for good.

So time passed, I became a full-fledged grocery clerk, and my wages rose from five rubles a semester to twenty-five. But collecting these princely wages was sometimes another matter. In Columbus's country, of course, wages are paid by check; sometimes, it is true, by checks with rubber feet, which bounce back, but at least it's all nice and respectable, with deductions for Social Security, and all the rest of it. With us, when payday came, it nearly always ended in a fight, because the clerk remembered he'd been promised *this* sum, and the boss firmly remembered they'd agreed on a much smaller one.

Usually, the boss prevailed, and the clerk's only recourse was to quit his job. This wasn't always such a wise move, because often the quality of the room and board was far more important than the wages.

I had one job where the food wasn't bad, but you slept on the floor and used your arm for a pillow. Another offered a respectable iron bed with a straw mattress, but the food was almost nonexistent. Now it is well-known that no one gets tired of bread. But what if even that is not put before you until your tongue is hanging out? This boss had a house full of children who somehow had been trained to demand food only every other day, and I, of course, had no choice but to learn how to do the same.

Now, the first day when I saw the boss forget to give me breakfast, I figured he'd make up for it at lunch. But when the afternoon went by with neither sight nor sound of food, I began to wonder if perhaps he'd hired me for a scientific experiment, to see how long the human body can live on water alone.

It's true I got something to eat that evening, but after a couple of weeks on such a remarkable diet, I began spitting blood, and some kind neighbors advised me that I had a thing called tuberculosis. I ran to my sleepy brother the baker, and he wrote my parents, and my mother arrived and took me to a doctor.

This Dr. Hertz needed to examine me for only a minute to find that I was not tubercular, but simply suffering from a disease called malnutrition. The only medicine he prescribed was for me to quit my job at once.

My boss's wife was astonished. She said she couldn't understand my reason for leaving. Hadn't she fed me as well as she had fed her own children? This may well have been true.

Of course, the best time to go hunting for a new job was in September, when all the twenty-one-year olds who weren't blessed with ruptures, lameness, blindness, loss of hearing, or some spectacular skin disease belonged to Czar Nicolai, may he rest in the ground. Sometimes a very good position thus might open up, and by now I was independent enough not to go job-hunting in person, but to send one of the professional "agents" you saw hanging around the cafés.

Thus it was that I obtained the last of my jobs before I became a full-time professional labor agitator. I remember this last job so clearly because it was the only one that didn't drain me of all my energy, and thus very nearly led me to fall into the very temptation our father Joseph had so nobly resisted with Potiphar's wife that in our scriptural reading of the event, a triple emphasis is placed upon the words, "and he refused."

I know that among American young men a pretty face is

taken as conclusive evidence that the temper of an angel rests behind it. For all I know, with American women that may be so. I would certainly not claim that only ugly women are good-natured.

But of all the jobs I held in Warsaw, the best paying and least comfortable was with a rich property owner who had a young and beautiful wife.

He needed a manager for some of his smaller properties, apartment houses, stores, and the like, and the job paid seventy-five rubles a semester, plus commissions, plus room and board.

Now I was used to "rooms," which meant sleeping on a straw sack in the cellar, and "board," which required talents a hunger-artist in a sideshow might have envied. But in this house the food was good, and I had a real bedroom to myself. The only trouble was that my little room was separated from that of my master and his wife by only a thin wall. And, plain and simple, it was impossible to sleep. The first night I was awakened by a violent crash. I thought the house had fallen in, until I realized with deep embarrassment that the master and his wife were having a little conversation with their fists. They were fighting about nothing of consequence—merely that for which even a Jew is permitted to shed blood—once.

To me, this made no sense at all. How could a normal man raise his hand to such an angel of a woman? And how could a husband and wife hit one another without saying a word? Respectable people, when they fight, they also yell, they curse, they *express* themselves. This fighting in bitter silence seemed somehow indecent to me.

At first I thought they kept quiet only out of consideration for me in the next room. But I soon found out that they alternated: sometimes, they fought without saying a word; other times, they quarreled and cursed each other without striking a blow.

I would have quit immediately, but for one thing: the master's wife. She was a blond little darling with a delightful figure and the face of a china doll, and I strongly suspected that she was the kind who starts laughing even before you tickle her.

But from these delicious little hands there flew an almost daily succession of missiles—a rolling pin, a grater, a teacup, a broom—all addressed to her unappreciative husband's head.

Sometimes I would enter a room unawares and intercept one of these flying expressions of love with my own hard head. But she always apologized instantly with such sweet language and demeanor, assuring me that she would never dream of hurting me, but only him, her heart's desire. I only wished she would hit me more often. At times I even purposely burst into a room where the battle was raging, in hopes of becoming a treasured casualty once again.

Her husband, after some years of this exciting marriage, had developed such an acrobatic cunning in the way he avoided her missiles that I think Charlie Chaplin could have taken lessons from him. Not that this warfare went on all the time. They had approximately two weeks of cease-fire for every two weeks of fighting, which I understood had to do with a woman's biological peculiarities, or the tides of the moon, or some such mystery.

But, much as I admired the master's wife, half the time the atmosphere in that house was so poisonous that I began to understand why he paid such good wages and yet was unable to keep his help. During the two weeks of war, his wife saw to it that all the delicacies the cook prepared for the husband ended up in my mouth instead. She would sit with me at her own table, and complain of how her swine of a husband ran after other women, which to me was truly incomprehensible. If I had a wife like that, I thought, I would have carried her on my hands.

What could I do but sympathize and eat, and eat and sympathize? But when she and her husband were at peace again, I existed for her no more than the dirt on the stairs. How true is the saying, "Better an ugly wife who is yours than the greatest beauty in another man's bed." And so, out of simple jealousy, I finally was able to summon up the strength to quit.

It was this last job which finally decided me on the career of a labor organizer. Although I was already close to the age for conscription, I felt there was no future for me in being a clerk, a stock boy, or even a manager. From now on, instead of working for the bosses, I would throw my youthful energies into the cause of the oppressed workers.

With a hard-boiled Lithuanian bundist to show me the ropes, I went to work as a paid professional, trying to organize the young bakers, grocery clerks, butchers, and even shoemakers, whose laughable wages, frankly, were greater than mine. The bundist encouraged me by pointing out that, where he came from in Vilna, the *dead* had more initiative than the workers in Warsaw. To my amazement, I managed to "unionize" over 3,000 workers in less than a month.

At the risk of their jobs and residence permits, they came to us because they felt they had nothing to lose. There was no need at all to bother their heads or mine with theories and ideology. In fact, as far as our political orientation was concerned, I couldn't tell you if it was Left or Right. And ideology wasn't the only thing we lacked. Young as I was, I had a good knack for agitating, making speeches, and signing up members, but none at all for strategy or administration. At first, this didn't worry me too much. After all, as the saying goes, Lemberg wasn't built in a day.

Also, in its initial phase, what hampered our work was not my lack of executive ability. It was the police, who soon began to harass me at every turn, who arrested me several times, beat me up once or twice, and threatened me with deportation. Fortunately, although they had me on their list as some kind of political troublemaker, they never quite figured out exactly what I was up to, either because they had had no experience with labor agitators, or because they couldn't imagine one to be as young as I.

But finally I was summoned to our so-called union headquarters and told I had to go underground. How? By taking a job in a store once again. It seemed that the police were beginning to catch on to what I was doing, and the organization considered me too valuable to lose.

Without much enthusiasm, I went to work for a sugar whole-saler, and at once found myself back among the very conditions I'd been fighting against. There were twelve workers, three of whom had enough seniority to rate beds with blankets. The rest of us slept on sugar sacks, also inhabited by bedbugs and various other of God's creatures whom the sugar attracted.

After two nights of no sleep, I gave up and moved to a hotel. Mornings I reported for work at the same time as the others, and, like them, spent the day looking forward to "dinner," the only meal our boss felt obligated to set before us. This normally con-sisted of a large pot of water in which a few carefully counted grains of kasha had been drowned.

For preparing this repast the boss employed not one but two cooks. One of these was a dirty girl who dragged herself around all day scratching her disheveled head. The other was a deaf and quarrelsome old woman whose husband had run away.

Our two cooks were bitterly jealous of one another, and did everything at cross-purposes. If one cook forgot to put salt into the kasha, you could count on the other one to forget as well. The next day, in response to our complaints, *both* would put salt into the boiling water, and the boss's wife, remembering our previous dep-rivation, also added a generous handful. About this diet you could truly say, "If you're hungry, lick salt—and you'll be thirsty in-stead."

I lived like this for a while, and realized that all of our organizing had accomplished absolutely nothing for the workers. If I stayed here, I'd soon be spitting blood again, which frightened me more than the police spies.

One morning I went in to the boss and told him that I and his three best clerks were quitting. I had hoped for a mass resigna-tion, but the others were like those broken-spirited Hebrew slaves who were afraid to leave the fleshpots of Egypt.

The boss was furious, of course. He accused me of being a Bolshevik, a hooligan, a nihilist, a spoiled young man who'd never be satisfied with anything short of total chaos, anarchy, and the destruction of the social order. It was impossible to make him see that no one can work without eating or sleeping. Not because I lacked eloquence, but because the remaining employees proved to him that there were people who could.

In the end, I got angry too, and instead of merely quitting I called a strike, and demanded not simply an improvement in the food and bedding but—and this was really unheard of in Warsaw —a reduction of the working day from eighteen hours to twelve.

To my astonishment, our little strike began to spread like spilled water. Without any efforts at organization on my part, workers and apprentices all over Warsaw began walking out and demanding a seventy-two-hour week. Of course, the great majority of workers stayed at their jobs because, like some of our slave ancestors, they were so accustomed to working day and night, to sleeping on sacks and eating salted water, they'd begun to believe there is nothing better to be had in the world.

So we had to adopt measures, or what today you would call "terrorism." Windows were broken and scabs were beaten up or their work sabotaged. At one bakery we ruined all the dough by mixing kerosene into it. At another place we sent pickets to remove two nonstrikers from a grocery store. But, since the scabs couldn't be found, the pickets beat up the bosses instead. The police, as usual, arrived long after it was all over and arrested two innocent yeshivah boys walking by with *tefillin* bags under their arms.

In general, though, I must admit that the strike went like a ship without a rudder. No one had any idea of tactics or of a negotiating position on what we might be willing to settle for. And certainly no one was going to take orders from a boy of twenty.

The result was that the strike dragged on for a while, growing steadily weaker, until gradually each boss came to some sort of quiet arrangement with his workers. It was like a husband and wife deciding it's better to live together in hatred than to have your self-respect and lie in the street.

One morning I woke up to find myself a strike leader without a strike to lead. The proper thing, no doubt, would have been for us union officials to attempt persuasion, or still more "terrorism," until the workers walked back out and the bosses were brought to their knees. But no one, including myself, was in a mood to start all over again. So our leadership consoled itself with the illusion that although we hadn't achieved our goal of a seventy-two-hour week this time, we had, after all, shaken Warsaw to its very foundations and triumphantly succeeded in giving countless thousands of workers a sense of revolutionary consciousness.

10. How to Become the Czar's Son-in-law

Every year, with the declining days of Elul, a familiar pall of fear began to descend on our village. Soon it would once again be the 15th of September. It was a date which struck a shudder even in the breasts of mothers who were still suckling their sons, for on that day all the young men who had reached military age during the year became subject to immediate conscription.

Do I need to paint you a picture of what it meant in 1902, particularly for a Jew, to be pitchforked into the Czar's army? Our elders' terror of conscription, though, was due only in part to the knowledge that we would be exposed to certain dangers and discomforts, not to mention being subject to the mercies and whims of superiors who would as soon torment a Jew as scratch themselves. Inconveniences like that were, after all, not exactly unknown even here in Vishogrod, among one's own good Polish neighbors. What Jewish parents dreaded above all was the prospect, amply shown to be a reality by returning soldiers, of sons who, within less than four years, would come home coarsened, brutalized, Russianized, and, in short, with scarcely a spark of human (that is, Jewish) feeling still left in them.

Thus, as the summer dwindled to an end every other home rang with heated family conferences, all dedicated to the search for some means by which an innocent child could be preserved from the fatal clutches of Fonya's army.

For the rich, there was no problem. You bought your way out. To the poor, however, there was only one avenue of escape: self-mutilation. And since there were any number of equally frightful possibilities to choose from, long evenings of consultation took place.

The year my turn arrived, Aunt Tzivia strongly recommended a man who would draw out all my teeth. Feibush the bath attendant held that the surest remedy would be for me to blind myself in my right eye, the one without which a man cannot aim a rifle. And my Uncle Yonah, never at a loss, knew a man skilled in the art of severing a tendon at the knee.

None of these schemes, I am glad to say, found favor with my parents. In fact, the only suggestion they considered as not totally devoid of sense was the one proposed by Zanvel the matchmaker, who held that, for an unmarried young man, the most respectable disability was a hernia, which afterwards could be hidden easily from prospective in-laws.

Had I accepted even half the suggestions offered to me, I should not only have escaped military service, but I would have ended up a cripple such as the world had never seen.

(The biggest joke of all, as I read years later, was that at this very time the proportion of Jews in the Russian army and navy was almost forty percent greater than its proportion of the population. The reason for this I'll leave to greater philosophers than I to figure out.)

Although no one had bothered to ask *me*, I hadn't the slightest intention of maiming myself. In fact, the prospect of becoming the Czar's *eidem oyf kest* for three years and eight months did not, frankly, strike me as the world coming to an end.

Meanwhile, though, in anticipation of my finding some way

to avoid conscription, our little house had also come to life with matchmakers. These, I am flattered to say, considered me a good bargain despite whatever self-inflicted disability I might come up with. Not that Jewish girls in the early 1900s didn't have standards as high as anyone else's. But, unlike their Hollywood-crazed sisters of today, they were not quite so stuck on physical perfection. In fact, you must forgive me, but such girls as we had in Vishogrod just don't exist any longer. Compared to what you see here today in Columbus's country, our girls had never grown pale, dusty, and gaunt from drudging in sweatshops, riding on subways crushed like raisins, or squandering half the night at dances that improve your health as little as your marital prospects.

Ordinarily, of course, I would not have run the risk of giving qualified approval to almost everything the matchmakers threw at me. But I felt reasonably certain that the Czar would rescue me before I had to make any life-or-death decisions.

Altogether, that year our village had fifty-four young men eligible for conscription, excluding those, Jew or gentile, who had already disabled themselves or bought exemptions. And since, for us, while awaiting September 15th, there no longer seemed to be much point in working or studying, the village rang nightly with the noise of furious celebration. Fully aware that Fonya would be starving us soon enough, we tried to fortify and anesthetize ourselves with orgies of eating and drinking.

Where did we get the money for our feasts? The fact is, there were certain traditional ways for boys in our tragic and privileged position to raise funds. As in previous years, the prospective Jewish conscripts had organized themselves into a committee, elected a treasurer, a *gabbai*, and a secretary, and impudently leveled a tax on the more fortunate of our fellow Jews.

We came and said to them, quite simply, "You're staying home, while we are off to serve the Czar." There is no need to remind me that even such an innocent remark, if delivered by a couple of healthy young men in a somewhat reproachful tone, was what any American lawyer, without charging you for the advice, would call criminal extortion. But you must understand that the money we collected wasn't spent on food and drink alone. Going into Fonya's army was not only a personal sacrifice, it also required a cash investment. Each recruit needed at least twenty-five rubles for such necessities as boots, socks, and a strong sheepskin coat, none of which the Czar was accustomed to lavish upon his defenders. In addition, those who did not intend to touch Fonya's unclean food until they absolutely had no choice also had to stock up on things like bread, chicken fat, and sausages.

I remember the first victim we called on was Meyer, the retired blacksmith. His well-kept beard smelled of scholarship and piety, although in truth he was an utter ignoramus and a bad Jew, who had never been guilty of giving a kopek to a charitable cause.

(Not giving to charity in our village was a far more serious business than it is today. Almost fifty percent of all Jewish families were able to make *Shabbos*, not to mention Pesach, only by grace of the handouts they received. A man who didn't give almost literally doomed another man to starvation.)

Meyer, at our demand for seventy-five rubles, started to bewail the bad times, and, getting nowhere with that, abruptly offered to settle with us for thirty-five. We refused to bargain. In the end, we came away with a pledge of seventy-five rubles, and an immediate cash advance of twenty-five. But on our way out, he called us back to complain that the father of one of the boys owed him three rubles. Couldn't he at least deduct that from our seventy-five? We coldly informed him that his private debts were his own problem.

From most other householders we only asked five or ten rubles, and sometimes even less than that. Altogether, we collected more than enough to outfit all the conscripts. With the balance, we had a few more good parties, and whatever money was left over by September 15th we gave to the Rabbi to distribute to the poor.

I don't mean to give the impression it was all that easy to intimidate some of our neighbors. After all, being Jews, no matter what *we* could do to them, they'd seen worse. And so, even some of those who should have been most grateful to us for filling the conscription quota didn't see what right we had to go about collecting money.

What did we do in such cases?

There was, for example, Yankel the teamster, who owned six horses and was childless and, above all, charged interest on money he lent to other Jews. Yankel recently had bought a new coach, of which he was as proud as a father of a new son. Part of our town, as I may have mentioned, was situated on the side of a hill. So one dark night, half a dozen of us applied our shoulders to the coach after releasing the brake, and pushed it until it faced downhill. From there, with the merest little nudge, it continued by its own momentum on down into the valley, where its wreckage may be lying to this day.

Kokoshka the tailor also held himself to be too good to respond to our appeal. Consequently, one morning when he got up he found his front door mysteriously sealed by a gigantic boulder which our boys had rolled against it during the night. After raising a tremendous cry to be let out and being informed of the price, Kokoshka paid his tax through the window, and it took all our strength to remove the stone from his door again.

If you think our methods were unduly severe for good Jewish boys, you will be reassured to know that the gentile conscripts in our town were no less brutal in imposing a similar sort of levy on their people. But, being neither as organized nor as inventive as ourselves, all they could think of to punish reluctant donors was to tear the crucifixes off their walls or release the pigs from their sties.

I know you've been waiting to ask, where were the police in all this? First of all, there were only two of them. One, who was also the mayor, was a Russian at least eighty-five years old who had very nearly forgotten his own language and communicated with his citizens only in pure Yiddish and broken Polish.

The second was said to be a descendant of Cantonists, those

pitiful Jewish children who, under Nicolai I, often used to be literally kidnapped at the age of eight or ten for twenty-five years of military service—counted from their eighteenth birthday, if they lived until then. He was an ancient, harmless, crook-backed little man whose sunken chest barely managed to support two corroded medals, earned for Heaven knows what acts of bravery during the first half of the previous century.

He normally made himself useful by emptying troughs, chopping wood, or shepherding someone's goat to the meadow. Perversely, the one service you couldn't prevail upon him to perform was to stoke an oven on *Shabbos*. From this it was concluded that he must have had at least a Jewish father, who, like so many Cantonists, had been forcibly converted as a child.

Presently, of course, the dreaded moment arrived.

On the 15th of September we climbed into a row of open wagons and, with a good deal of comradely passing of vodka between Jew and gentile, we jolted toward Plotsk, the capital of the *gubernya* (county).

By ten o'clock the following morning I was at the induction center, mother-naked, for a medical examination by several army doctors who fell all over themselves to pronounce me fit, and even wanted to know, "Where do we find more young men like this?"

Meanwhile, the brief, drunken friendship between the young Jews and Poles from our home town already had come unstuck. In the room in which we put our clothes back on, a brawl had developed over some remarks passed on the sacred subject of circumcision. Though my role in the fight was relatively modest, I ended up with a mashed finger which had gotten caught in someone's teeth.

Together with a friend who also had sustained some damage, I went to the aid-station, where, by luck, we happened to meet our future company clerk. This little man took pleasure in giving us advance notice that we were to be stationed deep in Siberia, a province not legendary for its temperate climate.

What to do? Without parents or relatives to advise us, we

didn't know the first thing about whom to bribe, even if we had had sufficient money in our pockets. We therefore decided, since our company was not to be shipped out for another couple of days, to absent ourselves and go home for *Shabbos.*

Once more we hitchhiked for a day and a half in such a downpour as might have swamped Noah's ark. Worst of all, for the last half-dozen kilometers, as the sky began to darken for the Sabbath, we had to walk, and finally to run, for if it were past candle-lighting time when we arrived in the village, it would be obvious, to our parents' disgrace, that Fonya's army, in less than a day, already had turned us into heathens.

Although our lungs rattled with the strain, we were unable to reach the village until well after the synagogues had emptied.

But when at last I came to our little house and looked into the window, I suddenly felt unable to cross the threshold. I was a Russian soldier now, no longer one of *them,* and when they saw me they would surely burst into tears at my misfortune, and their *Shabbos* would be ruined.

So I stood at the window, shivering in the deep mud, and stared at the dear, honorable features of my father, as he sang his familiar *zmiros,* and watched the sympathetic flicker of the candles as my mother quietly wept to herself. My father suddenly stopped singing and admonished her, "We are forbidden to mourn on the Sabbath." But my mother's weeping continued. "If at least he were here today, for one last *Shabbos.*" And at those words I saw even my father shed a tear.

I couldn't stand it any longer. I burst into the house and cried, "Good *Shabbos!*" My mother fell upon my neck and drenched me with her tears. But my father had already regained his self-control. Bidding me *"sholom aleichem,"* he asked no questions, but handed me a *siddur* to catch up with the evening prayers I had missed. He wanted it clearly understood that being a soldier of the Czar did not absolve one from one's daily duty as a soldier of the Almighty.

After *Shabbos* I told my parents why I had returned. What

could be done to change my orders so that I would not have to go to Siberia?

All the great advice-givers who had been so full of ingenious schemes for self-mutilation were silent now. Only the Rabbi had a diffident suggestion. Perhaps an emissary should be sent in person to the military governor at Plotsk. What sort of an emissary? The Rabbi hesitated to say. But we understood what he meant. Better a woman than a man. And better a young woman than an old one.

Now we had in our town a girl named Malkah, twenty-three years old, tall, high-bosomed, with raven hair and fiery coal-black eyes, altogether a veritable Queen Esther. Among her family and friends she was known as "Malkah Cossack," not for any fierceness of temper but because of the quickness of her wit. This, we felt, would be sufficient to deflate any *notchalnik*, any official, trying to take advantage of her. Malkah readily agreed to go and intercede for me. Why? Because Malkah Cossack was none other than my own sister.

She left for Plotsk early the following morning.

The gist of her appeal there, as she told us on her return, was, "We are loyal subjects of the divinely appointed Czar, and already have the unspeakable privilege of an older son serving him in Petersburg. We could hardly wait for his brother to attain military age. And now that we have had the good fortune to see him accepted for service to the holy Czar, nothing could make our happiness more complete than to know the two brothers are reunited, serving shoulder to shoulder."

It didn't all go one-two-three, but in the end, the *notchalnik*, his eyes glittering with gentlemanly charm, pressed Malkah's hand perhaps longer than necessary and assured her, "Your request shall at once be granted."

It was, of course, not possible for me to stay and find out if he'd kept his word. The time had come for me to leave, as Scripture puts it, my land, my place of birth, and my father's house. In yet another driving rainstorm (do I remember no sunny days at all?), I left for Plotsk with my soldier's baggage. This amounted mainly to a canvas-covered box, which my mother had filled with bread, herring, chicken fat, and sausages. Accompanying me to the coach were not only my near and distant relatives, but acquaintances who seemed to have come solely for the purpose of adding their tears to the puddles made by the rain.

My father alone expressed his sorrow by remaining silent. But it was only *his* three parting words that continued to ring in my ears long after the coach had taken me away. All he had said was, "Be a Jew."

11. A Small Cheer for Corruption

So instead of immediately being sent somewhere into the black depths of Siberia, as were most of the boys from our village that year, even including some of the gentiles, I was posted to St. Petersburg, where my older brother Mordechai was stationed and, judging by his own vague accounts, apparently had attained a position of some influence.

But, as though to rub it in that my body and soul no longer belonged to our Father in Heaven, but to our Little Father the Czar, my orders were to leave from Warsaw at eight o'clock on a *Shabbos* morning, and even my father understood that this was a matter of breaking the Sabbath only because one's life was at risk.

As our barge rocked along the Vistula under a weeping sky, I could for a while still faintly glimpse the nebulous hills of my birthplace and, with the sudden sharp realization that soldiers don't always return alive, I wondered if I should ever see it again.

Crowded below deck on account of the rain, we stood in steamy, suffocating closeness—Jew and Pole, Balt, Ukrainian, and transplanted German—and although the recent Syedlitzer pogrom was still green in our memories, we managed somehow not to be at each others' throats. This may have been because, for the moment, our common fate had imposed a temporary truce on us. Or, this being 1902, because few young people had remained untouched by the prevailing revolutionary spirit, with its rosy premonitions of universal brotherhood.

Not counting my own special case, most of the young men chosen for duty in Petersburg were the tallest and handsomest of each village, fit for the Czar's own household troops and body-guard; the kind who, as the saying goes, "could dance right off your plate."

Some time around noon (determined not by the absent sun but by the hunger pangs in our bellies) the barge stopped and we were marched, in a straggling column of twos, to a railway siding, where we boarded a passenger train. Although it was unheated, we could at least sit down.

While waiting for the train to start, and sharing a bottle of vodka providentially carried by one of the Polish boys, a Fonya noncom with a stripe on his collar came pushing in with a stack of papers and started calling our names.

Having, to his visible astonishment, found us all accounted for, he now launched into a pompous sermon on how we should conduct ourselves as good, pious subjects of the Czar, meaning we were to jump to obey all of *his* orders. In the meantime, we would shortly be issued our subsistence pay.

My one friend in the group, Glasnik, a skeptical boy from Warsaw, whispered into my ear in Yiddish, "What's the heathen jabbering about?"

"He's speaking Russian."

"What's he saying?"

"He's got money for us."

"Why didn't he steal it? Who would know?"

"Ask *him.*"

"Fonya *gonnef.* This one looks too dumb even to be a thief."

Presently the train started up and, before my skeptical friend could wonder if it was the right train, and not some cattle express bound for Manchuria, another Fonya walked into our car bearing a sack of coins. Now, of course, I knew already that the Czar didn't pay princely wages. But even I was unprepared to be handed seven groschen for a day's subsistence, which at that time was not quite enough to buy a pound of bread.

There was a roar of protest, which the second Fonya tried to appease by pointing out that at each stop we would also get free hot water.

Among those who raged against this "Russian thievery" some of the gentile Polish boys (raised to believe that Poland was *their* country and not a Russian colony) were particularly incensed, and the two noncoms seemed on the verge of being overwhelmed by a spontaneous uprising.

I, for my part, wanted nothing to delay or prevent my getting to Petersburg, and tried to calm down the Poles by pointing out that it was undoubtedly not the noncoms who were robbing us, but the really great thieves at the top, who took the money allotted for soldiers' food and put it into their own pockets.

I never would have dreamt I'd said anything out of line, except that the two noncoms I had saved from a taste of hearty Polish violence asked me gratefully for my name, and then let me know they'd have their eye on me now as a revolutionary agitator. Following which they began to bless us all impartially with good Russian benedictions, and ended up with the assurance that there was an excellent chance the lot of us, without exception, would end up sampling the inside of a prison fortress for attempted mutiny.

I must admit that by this time being a soldier of the Czar had lost much of its charm for me. I resolved for the balance of my enlistment to keep my nose out of all brawls, mutinies, riots, or revolutions, or, in fact, any incidents other than those involving what I grandly thought of as "the honor of the Jewish people."

After a couple of hours, the train left Poland and, in the gloom of a sunless afternoon, began its grudging progress through a desolate landscape of meager fields, occasionally populated by skinny Russian horses and skeletal cows hunting for blades of grass. The Russians, I thought, might be a great military power, but they had a lot to learn about farming.

Night fell, and the train sped on, without one stop for the promised hot water, while the lot of us scratched our unwashed bodies and groped peevishly for comfortable positions in which to sleep. Finally, in the suffocating air and the foul smell of our bodies and feet, most of us fell into a state which was not so much sleep as loss of consciousness.

It seemed to me that I had barely closed an eye, when the train screamed and shuddered to a halt. The time was shortly after midnight. Military voices roared at us to get off with all of our belongings. We tumbled out, still only half-awake, and were driven like cattle through narrow, dirty streets until we reached a row of barracks.

Here, in the mess hall, were a row of long tables hammered together out of splintery boards. On each table was placed a tin bowl filled with cooked dirty water. Floating desperately on top of this 'brew were a few scraps of roasted pigskin which had probably been too tough to make into boots.

We were each given one of the Russian army's famous wooden spoons. But while the others fell upon this soup as though it were fresh-baked bread, none of the Jews in our group tasted a drop. Not that we wouldn't, eventually, have to eat the same unclean food as everyone else. But each of us put off that moment as long as he could.

At two in the morning, we were herded back to the station. Along the way, our comrades discussed their first military supper. One said it was perhaps a little too salty; another complained there wasn't enough fat in it; a third guessed that the cook had washed his dirty clothes in the water; and a fourth agreed that the soup did have a slight taste of army soap. And all of them roundly cursed Fonya for his stinginess with food.

In the morning, they loaded us into boxcars that had signs

advising that occupancy was limited to eight horses or forty men. Two days later, at four in the morning, we reached Petersburg. It had been arranged by telegram that my brother Mordechai would meet me at the station. He was, after all, no ordinary soldier but a big-shot corporal in the Quartermaster Corps, and had some freedom of movement. But, to my great disappointment, he was not there. (It turned out afterwards that he had already been to the station several times, and had even brought a small welcoming committee. In fact, the very morning I arrived, he had just gone back to his barracks because the stationmaster, with that wonderful Russian efficiency even the Communists could never change, had told him the train was not due until the next day.)

At the station, no one had prepared for our arrival with even a caldron of tea. The first snows of the winter had just fallen. Through this we trudged at dawn with our belongings, along endless Petersburg streets, for what seemed like a good five hours. Finally, panting and staggering with exhaustion and drenched with sweat, we reached the Novocherkassky Barracks.

Our feet were swollen, and a man would have needed an icepick before he could blow his nose. On top of which we were hungry as wolves, and our revolutionary spirits were at a pitch not to be reached again until 1904.

We were now chased into dark, slippery barracks and guarded like prisoners who might try to escape. Our patience, I must say, was very nearly at an end, and we started to yell, "We want food." One boy hollered, "I want cabbage!" Another screamed, "I want sausage!" And, as long as the others were ordering their menu, Glasnik shouted, "I want gefilte fish and kugel!"

I must admit that, on this occasion, Fonya treated us all, Jew and gentile, with perfect equality. None of us got a thing. One of our guards explained they could give us no food because our names were not yet on the roster. They did, however, give us free hot water, and I for one was relieved to hear nothing more mentioned about our "mutiny" on the train.

Later we were all measured like yard goods, so that we might be assigned to platoons in a way that would best make use of our talents. Toward this end, we were also asked our civilian occupations. I gave mine, as my brother's letter had advised, as tailor, although I had never threaded a needle in my life. (Mordechai no doubt was afraid that, in my youthful stupidity, I would say "labor organizer" or "terrorist.")

Now, I knew already from some of the veterans back home that there was all the difference in the world between getting into a good platoon and a bad one. A good platoon meant sitting in an office and being part of *notchalstva*, officialdom. A bad one was bitter as death.

The outcome was that, on account of my height (with no regard whatever to my qualifications as a tailor), I was put into the Fifteenth Company. This had the reputation of being the "convicts' company." From the first morning on, I understood why.

In other companies the men were treated in a fairly civilized way. That is, they were awakened at six, cleaned their floors and polished their boots and brass buttons until seven, and then were taken out into the waist-high snow and made to run for an hour.

With the Fifteenth they were less gentle. We were roused at four, driven out into the snow at five, and kept running until eight, by which time the others were already sitting comfortably at breakfast, which consisted of tea with sugar and chunks of shriveled bread.

Since I was healthy enough not to be among those who collapsed during our morning run, I still had not fully realized what I was in for during the next three years and eight months. But I soon received Czar Nicolai's proper *sholom aleichem*, and that sobered me a little.

What happened was this. Not having tasted hot food for three days now, because some clerk had not yet gone to the trouble of putting our names on the roster, I got up early the second morning with a powerful thirst and took my own little teakettle over to the cookhouse.

The mess attendant explained he was not allowed to give out

any hot water until the bugle had sounded. I slipped him a cigarette. After all, if you wish to ride in comfort, you must grease the wheels.

I got my hot water and ran happily back to my cot to drink my tea. I was about to pour the first cup, when a Ukrainian noncom with a face like a sheep and a nose like a bulldog—the kind of treasure whom, in Russian Yiddish, we'd call a *katzap*—entered the barracks. Reading from an ominous roster in his hand, he asked for "Marateck, Yakub."

When I answered him, he took one shocked look at my cheerfully steaming kettle and promptly gave me a "Russian *misheberach,*" that is, a blow across the face which sent me sprawling.

Blood-spattered and stunned, I had barely managed to get back on my feet when he screamed, "Jewface, pick up your hand and salute!"

Until he said that, I had been willing to overlook his bad manners. But you must remember I grew to manhood in a section of Warsaw where a man does not lightly, as the saying goes, let someone spit into his kasha. So, without thinking, I snatched up the full kettle and walloped him once across the head, and, while I was at it, also allowed my fist to find a resting-place on his broad nose. In the commotion that followed, with plenty of warm encouragement for both sides, he ended up on the bottom and I on top, while the blood from our mouths and noses mingled fraternally on the floor.

If I fought more ferociously than the occasion really called for, it may have been that I was simply expressing my general sense of smothered Jewish rage about the recent Syedlitzer pogrom, in which I had participated as a volunteer in the so-called Jewish Self-Defense. Ill-trained and virtually unarmed, we had put up a good fight but were unable to avert very much bloodshed.

Presently an ambulance arrived with an army doctor, and my opponent was carried out very handsomely on a stretcher. They had one ready for me, too, because my blood also was gushing with more freedom than I would have liked to admit. But, to emphasize that I had gotten the better of the exchange, I insisted on walking to the ambulance without help.

At the hospital, my injuries turned out to be hardly worth mentioning: a tooth knocked out by the first blow, and a finger cut to the bone by the sharp edge of my own smashed kettle. But they insisted on putting me to bed, so that my opponent, who, among other things, had lost part of his nose, should not suffer by comparison.

Here Mordechai finally found me at two o'clock the following morning. He'd brought his own little welcoming delegation of Jewish soldiers from our home town. But when he found out I had committed violence against a Russian of superior rank, Mordechai, in his loving anxiety over my ignorance and dimming prospects for survival, started to shout at me. He predicted that, unless I learned to control my "Polak temper," I would spend my army years going from one prison to another until I forgot what a Jew was.

I listened to him with respect. He was, after all, something of a big shot in Fonya's scheme of things. But only later did I find out what made him so important. He was in charge of the warehouse from which the men drew their uniforms. And since a man has to live, especially in Petersburg, which was then almost a kind of New York with all sorts of expensive temptations, it was fortunate that in the Quartermaster Corps, as my brother quickly found out, a man would have to have a heart of stone not to pick up some money on the side.

From the lowest rank to the very highest, everyone prospered in some way. As for my straitlaced brother, had he behaved like a fanatic and raised his nose at all the flagrant misdemeanors going on right under it, he would not only have been despised as a simpleton, but, for everyone else's protection, would have quickly been transferred to some distant infantry command, if not worse.

The way the *notchalniks* in the Quartermaster worked their racket was as follows. Each soldier was entitled to a new uniform once in three years. The old one was then supposed to be ripped apart and used for rags to wash the floors. But, as it happened, many of the old uniforms were still in good enough condition so that, if you merely cleaned them up and sewed in a new lining, you could sell them again, or even issue them in place of new ones. Believe it or not, there were large sums of money to be made out of these "resurrections," and everyone, from the colonel on down, had a lick of this juicy bone. Mordechai, contrary to what you may be thinking, was the only Jew in that entire operation. And I suspect they kept him only because, in the management of the warehouse itself, they needed at least one honest man.

So my brother went about burdened with money he couldn't send home without confessing to my father how he came by it. He knew that our father, for all his grinding poverty, would not have tolerated such sources of income for a moment, and Mordechai would have been forced to ask for a transfer.

But, having been away from our father's influence a little longer than I, he explained to me that whether money was tainted or not depended largely on what you did with it. And since Mordechai lacked any inclination for gambling, drinking, or whoring, all he could think of doing with this cursed wealth was to lend it to those of his officers who never could manage on what they had, or to buy vodka for his Russian comrades and superiors, who would lap it up, cross themselves, and wish him eternal life.

It mattered little to him that few of his officers ever repaid his favors or loans. As a practical man, he reasoned, what Jew in Fonya's army could ever know for certain when a little influence in the right place might not one day literally mean the difference between life and death? And thus, almost despite himself, my brother became a man of some influence.

One of Mordechai's best "customers," but one who acknowledged at least *some* vague obligation to pay him back, was his own captain. A relative of the Czar himself, Captain Mikhailoff of course was a wealthy man. Yet he knew nothing whatever about holding on to his money, and freely admitted that his army pay alone couldn't even have kept him in cigarettes. Like most Russian officers, he was a passionate card player, and whenever his luck turned sour, he would tiptoe into Mordechai's quarters in the dark of night like a drunkard fearful of waking his wife. He always unerringly found his way to my brother's bed, and Mordechai, still half-asleep, would automatically slip him a hundred or two.

We have a saying, "Lend money and you buy yourself an enemy." But this, as it turned out, did not apply to Mikhailoff. He proved, in fact, to be a truly good soul with a merciful heart, which of course led to slanderous rumors about his having had a Jewish mother.

The question now, however, was did Mordechai possess sufficient influence to keep me out of jail?

After all, in Fonya's army it was virtually unheard of for a blood-raw recruit, and a "Polak Jew" at that, to raise a hand in anger to a noncommissioned officer, regardless of provocation. My sentence on conviction, it was sadly agreed, could well have come to twenty years. What's more, there was the reputation of the other Jewish soldiers to consider. You know the expression, "When a gentile steals, you hang the thief; when a Jew steals, you hang the Jew."

Although Mordechai was still in the midst of scolding me, some of his friends now reminded him that I had, after all, defended the honor of the Jewish people. Had he forgotten how many Jewish recruits this sheepfaced Ukrainian had beaten and tormented in the past? One man now also recalled having heard him boast that, in a certain pogrom, he personally had killed two Jews.

At this, my blood was boiling again and I bravely announced that if I'd known this, I wouldn't have stopped until I had dispatched him to the Other World, prison or no prison.

This, of course, instantly rekindled Mordechai's anger, but I felt his raging at me was like that of a loving father, and I didn't take it too much to heart.

One of his friends now said to him, "All right, big shot. Let's see what connections you have at headquarters not to let this go any further."

Mordechai mumbled and grumbled that his supposed influence was severely limited, and that he didn't even know who to go to. His captain? He couldn't be sure. It seemed that the very idea of a Jew committing violence against a Russian of superior rank had too much of a "man bites dog" novelty to keep out of the local paper, and thus could not simply be hushed up. Further, knowing the Russian officer class a good bit better than I, Mordechai had genuine doubts about whether his considerable investments in good will over these past two years would actually prove negotiable.

In the end, needless to say, he came through for me. Captain Mikhailoff, it turned out, appeared genuinely glad of an opportunity to repay Mordechai's many favors. The case, unfortunately, had already attracted too much notoriety for him to be able to obtain a dismissal of the charges. But he assured Mordechai I had nothing to worry about, nor would I need to incur the expense of a lawyer, for he himself would defend me in person.

I naturally had no way of knowing whether he actually understood the nature of the crime with which I had been charged, or what kind of legal training qualified him to defend a soldier in a court-martial. But it did me no good whatever to suggest to Mordechai that, since it was *my* life, or at least my future for the next twenty or thirty years, which was going to be determined by this military court, perhaps I would be better off with a professional lawyer.

After all, as my brother pointed out, who was *I* to say no to a blood relative of the Czar?

But the day of the trial arrived and I still had not so much as set eyes upon my "defense attorney." The devil only knew how he intended to present my side of the case. Mordechai, in between biting his lips, shouted at me not to be such a worrier. He conceded that there were some grounds for uneasiness only when the trial actually had begun and there was still no sign of Mikhailoff. All Mordechai could say to reassure me was that he'd probably been drunk the night before and overslept.

Meanwhile, my accuser had entered the courtroom as though he personally were about to sit in judgment of me. I noted that the repairs on his nose and face had been carried out so artistically that, although he still bore a brotherly resemblance to a sheep, altogether he looked notably less ugly than before.

Mordechai and some of his friends sat in the back row, listening with at least outward calm as the prosecutor painted our little brawl as an outrage committed by me alone, an act of unprovoked savagery and insubordination which, unless punished so severely as to set an example even for future generations, surely would lead to a speedy and total breakdown of all military discipline and hence, inevitably, to the dreaded revolution—a word which, in those days, was an almost automatic invitation to a death sentence.

I could see right off that the judge was not exactly in my corner. Any minute now, I would be called upon to speak in my own defense. And what could I talk about? "Jewish honor"? The Syedlitzer pogrom?

I could already see myself blindfolded and tied to the stake, especially since my aristocratic defender, who finally had strolled in and taken his seat, one hand vainly attempting to comfort a throbbing brow, listened to the prosecutor like a man who couldn't wait to put this tedious performance behind him and get back to bed. How truly did the Psalmist say, "Put not your trust in princes."

But first the aggrieved sergeant himself took the stand, bearing his scars as officiously as though they were battle wounds. He delivered a good strong recitation on how I had attacked him, totally without provocation, in what he could only assume to be a Polak Jew's typical frenzy of rebellion against good Russian discipline.

With each minute he spent talking, I could almost see the judge adding yet another soldier to the firing squad. But what offended me above all was to hear no objection from the judge when my opponent referred to me once again as *zhydovska morda* (translation: "Jewface," except *morda* refers more precisely to the visage of an animal).

At this point, Mikhailoff, who until now had maintained a morose, hung-over, rather self-pitying silence, rose to my defense. Once he had found his feet, he straightened his body with remarkable steadiness. But to my horror, he did not seem quite certain who in the room was the defendant. Nor, once he had found me, in belated response to Mordechai's frantic wagging of his chin, did he pay the slightest attention to any of the charges laid against me. Instead, he launched into an impassioned attack on those noncoms who, by their unrestrained brutality and total disrespect for the proud traditions of the Imperial Army, had already turned Heaven-only-knew how many innocent and patriotic recruits into embittered revolutionaries against *his* relative, the holy Czar.

It seemed to me a speech he had long been eager to get off his chest, and I suspect he would have made the identical speech had I been on trial for blasphemy or for wetting my bed. Needless to say, the last thing I wanted at this moment was for the court to see me as an "embittered revolutionary."

But there was simply no stopping the man and, to my surprise, although my defender was plainly the sort of man who had more growing under his nose than inside his head, I saw the judge repeatedly nodding his respectful agreement. But that still did not begin to dispose of the crime for which I was standing trial.

Only when he had at last finished delivering himself of his heartfelt harangue and seemed almost ready to sit down again, did he briefly take note of what he labeled "the so-called defendant." True, he conceded, perhaps a more experienced soldier might have tried to moderate his righteous anger. But what I had done was, after all, so patently an attempt only to defend the honor and security of *his* relative, the Czar, Captain Mikhailoff simply failed to comprehend why it was *me* and not the other man who was on trial here.

Much as I wanted to agree with my defender, even I had to admit that his argument lacked logic, not to mention common sense.

But the judge, to my astonishment, showed himself to be totally persuaded by this line of reasoning. While I was let off with only the most gentle of reprimands, Pyotr, my opponent, who hadn't been accused of anything, suddenly found himself reduced in rank.

How much, if anything, this verdict cost my brother, he never let on. For all I knew, my advocate might even have defended me in all sincerity. But the outcome certainly made me a good deal more tolerant toward the all-pervasive atmosphere of corruption in the Russian army.

What was it, after all, but corruption which injected some measure of humanity into a system in which a man's life or feelings had no more value than yesterday's snow? Without this constant lubrication of the wheels, the most appalling injustices would have passed unnoticed, and men in positions of power might never have felt the slightest inducement to lift a finger for another soul.

Jews, in particular, whom the system was designed openly either to convert to Christianity or to grind into the dust, often were able to survive only because most of the time, Fonya, bless him, loved money in his pocket or vodka in his belly even more than he loved the sight of Jewish blood.

So today, when a lard-faced New York policeman comes into the store with an open palm, I find it hard to get as indignant as I should. After all, were not some of the bloodiest events in human history carried out by men who were altogether incorruptible?

12. The Litvaks

After some weeks of basic training in the so-called convicts' company (which Mordechai felt I was in danger of beginning to enjoy rather more than was proper for a boy of my refined family background), I found myself unexpectedly transfered to the regimental tailor shop after all.

Here, out of eight men, I think two were actually tailors, and therefore obliged to cover for all the rest of us. However, neither one complained, because it was apparent that we others must have had some pull with *notchalstva*, or we wouldn't be there.

But I soon realized that my years in the commercial jungles and newborn labor movement of Warsaw had almost totally destroyed my ability to cope with the blessings of idleness, at least on weekdays. Within less than a month, to my brother's dismay, I began to crave some other outlet for my youthful energies and thirst for adventure.

Finally, against Mordechai's vehement advice, I applied successfully for a transfer to the Fourteenth Company, which was under the command of my old defender, Captain Mikhailoff, the Czar's relative. It was, after all, peacetime, and, while life in the infantry might have been a little more strenuous than smoking my pipe in the tailor shop, being back among real soldiers was as exciting to me as going to a summer camp with all facilities for outdoor sports would be to an American child today.

My parents' (and Mordechai's) principal concern of course had been that, once I wore the Czar's uniform, I would not only be outwardly transformed, but—gorged on Fonya's swinish food, helplessly exposed to his lewd and heathenish ways, and obliged, week after week, to profane the Sabbath—I would, like so many tens of thousands before me, soon forget I had ever been such a thing as a Jew.

But, as it turned out, I suffered from precisely the opposite affliction. The Fourteenth Company consisted of 118 men, 42 of whom were Jews. (Not that Jews didn't try as hard as any other normal person to avoid falling into Fonya's clutches. But, unlike our gentile neighbors, we had far fewer places to hide, and the recruiters who came after us also demanded much heavier bribes, shrewdly suspecting that Jews place greater value on their children.)

In any event, the Fourth Platoon, to which Mordechai arranged to have me assigned (hoping, he said, at least to keep me out of further brawls and courts-martial) was almost totally Jewish. Its only conspicuous gentile was the platoon sergeant. He, however, spoke a fluent Yiddish, having lit the stoves in Jewish homes on the Sabbath as a young orphan. For this service, he used to receive a large piece of *challah*, which was apparently one of the few pleasant memories he had of his entire childhood.

For a Jew in Fonya's army, I could hardly have been better situated. Yet, I must tell you, I felt very much estranged in my new platoon. Why? Because most of my new comrades were not at all what I was accustomed to think of as Jews. What they were was Litvaks, Jews from Lithuania, and not only did they seem to me, in my Polish innocence, not to *look* like Jews, but at first I had such a hard time understanding their nasal, crabbed Yiddish, I preferred to converse with them in Russian. But my problems went deeper than that.

Back in Warsaw, you see, almost the only Litvak I had ever known was this professional labor organizer, a man as cold-blooded as any gentile, who had taught me how to arrange work stoppages, lockouts, strikes, acts of sabotage, and even how to intimidate (that is, beat up) such class enemies as strikebreakers and stony-hearted bosses.

Exposure to such a hard-boiled character had of course done little to erase my childish prejudices, born of such expressions as "I saw two Jews and a Litvak," or "a Litvak has a cross in his head" (based on the suspicion that the Litvak's rigorous emphasis on study and religious observance, without the Hasid's sense of mystical joy, would one day surely lead him to apostasy); either that or, on the ungenerous charge that a Litvak is so calculatingly pious, he repents even before he sins.

But the most painful social barrier between the Litvaks and me arose from the unhappy fact that—in contrast to myself, a runaway from yeshivah at age twelve—there wasn't one of these fellows who couldn't learn.

I don't mean just the Five Books of Moses with the commentaries of Rashi, with which, thank God, I was as familiar as a Jewish child nowadays is with the baseball scores. But the only "learning" my Litvak comrades considered worthy of the term was a total immersion in the labyrinths of the Babylonian Talmud, a body of work whose surface, as a child, I had barely scratched enough to remember the four "fathers" of civil torts, the rules governing a wife during her menstrual cycle, and the conditions under which a bill of divorcement had to be written and delivered—in other words, the sort of odds and ends that even the dullest of us managed to soak up out of the air we breathed.

Not so these Litvaks. To them, learning was a deadly serious business, which took precedence over all else. If military training threatened to interfere, they simply, almost absentmindedly, picked up "Esau's skills" so well, they could have their bodies doing one thing while their minds were grimly, joyously, concentrated on the *real* world.

For an adult observant Jew to have remained as unschooled as I, of course, was not merely a challenge to them, but a provocation, and, in their one-track-minded Litvak way, they were resolved to elevate me to their own level. Thus, for instance, one time while rushing to get ready for rifle inspection, I momentarily misplaced my watch, and one of the Litvaks found it.

Nu, nu, don't ask what I went through before they'd let me have it back. After all, how *could* they return my property until due determination had been made whether or not it constituted a "found object," that is, whether I had dropped it or deliberately put it down, and whether on private property or in the public domain, and what unique identifying marks, if any, I had placed upon it, and whether the loss of my watch was analogous to the legal fiction concerning lumber displaced by the tides of a river, and whether or not I could be reasonably supposed to have already "despaired" of finding my lost property—in which case it would have been rendered *hefker,* ownerless.

They were not being sadistic; they merely fell like hungry wolves upon the slightest pretext to relate their learning to a real-life situation.

Far from being brutalized or corrupted by Fonya's army, these wretched Litvaks, even at bayonet practice, on the rifle range, or on cross-country rides, would unreel talmudic pros and cons as lightly as a blacksmith hammering horseshoes. And they had yet another intolerable trait. Not one of them was descended from anything less than a rabbi. For no amount of money would you have found among them one man who would admit to descent from ordinary Jewish parents.

Worst of all, as my brother Mordechai resignedly pointed out to me, they were probably telling the truth. Their part of Lithuania indeed was renowned as a district where, as they say, even a dog could "learn," and every Jew was as steeped in ancestral merit as a pig is steeped in mud.

Among the other Jewish soldiers in my company, there were two kinds. The ones with whom, to my surprise, I had the least in common were those who had made up their minds to do as little as possible for the hated czarist regime. Not, however, for any good revolutionary reasons. They simply didn't feel the Czar had any business drafting *them*. By their conduct, these fellows naturally "blackened the faces" of *all* Jewish soldiers because, no matter how well the rest of us did, some of our comrades, not to mention officers, grasped every chance to judge us all by the actions of these few.

Altogether, our company had three of these treasures. One of them nightly bepissed his bed until his straw mattress began to rot, and none of us could bear to sleep in the same room with him. He finally was examined by a medical commission, which ruled that his bladder was perfectly in order, and that if he continued his disgusting practices, his comrades should feel free to take their own measures. Since this was an order we all were ready to obey with great enthusiasm, our leaking comrade promptly made a miraculous recovery and in time even developed into quite a decent soldier.

The second one went on a hunger strike the day he left home, limiting himself to bread and water, and of course he soon was too weak even to get out of bed. The rest of us begged him not to undermine Jewish honor. If he had scruples against touching food cooked in Fonya's tainted pots, we would give him money to buy cabbage, potatoes, tea, sausage. But it turned out that his refusal of hot food was not on anything as principled as religious grounds. It was simply that he had read somewhere that a man who goes without eating anything warm for three months will develop rheumatism and be eligible for a discharge.

But when, after twelve weeks of suffering, he was still as far from rheumatism as I am from Paris, while seeing that Fonya's doctors were perfectly content to see him die of starvation rather than send him home, he, too, quietly abandoned his medical experiment and began to eat like a human being again. In the end, we had reason to be satisfied with his soldiering, too.

But there was a third recalcitrant in our company who did manage to get out. He happened to be a cantor, at least so he told us, and none of us had ever been in his home town to prove otherwise. Only this cantor's conduct would have been more becoming for an ordinary Communist, for he brazenly stuffed himself with pork, smoked on the Sabbath, and pushed himself among the commonest sort of women.

I once asked him how fitting he thought it was for a cantor, who is called "the congregation's intermediary," to behave like such a swine.

He replied, in a parody of a talmudic singsong, that what he did was perfectly proper. "After all, on the Days of Awe, before the Additional Service, does not the cantor publicly say of himself, '. . . for a sinner and transgressor am I, and may the congregation not be shamed on account of my own unfitness.' Therefore, if I did not conduct myself as I did, then on the holiest of days, when required publicly to admit my unworthiness, I would be lying to the Almighty." (This, I am sorry to tell you, was *also* an example of Litvak reasoning.)

Anyway, this cantor's habit was to stuff himself with up to nine pounds of bread per day, until the officer in charge of provisions reported his outrageous appetite to the regimental commander, who convened another medical commission. These doctors demanded to know why the cantor ate so much bread. He explained that he was always hungry and, if he ate any less, he would not have sufficient strength to do his duty.

In the end, the commission, in its wisdom, decided he was suffering from tapeworm and they actually sent him home.

Of course, from a purely *political* point of view, I should have been in full sympathy with anyone who saw no reason to exert himself on behalf of a Czar who, like some of his ancestors, was restrained only by indolence or absentmindedness from putting an end to us all. But my own attitude was, as long as you're compelled to serve Fonya, why not rub it under his nose how good a soldier a Jew could be—if he felt like it? And it griped me when I overheard my Russian comrades use those few slackers as an excuse for remarks about Jews who were serving only because they'd been too cowardly to obtain exemption by shooting themselves in the foot.

Of course, the best answer to such crude remarks, aside from an instant bloody nose, came from that group of Jews in our regiment who were neither hair-splitting Litvaks nor passive resisters. These boys were, in fact, a wild, brawling, hard-drinking lot, such as any army would have been glad to have. Take Brodsky, son of a Kiev millionaire, who was the best horseman in the regiment. In competitions, he beat not only the Cossacks but even the Circassians, men who virtually were born in the saddle. One of Brodsky's favorite tricks (which, after a good many falls and bruises, I eventually learned to imitate) was to stand in a field, with his horse half a mile away. The horse would come galloping at him at full speed and, as it passed Brodsky, there he'd suddenly be in the saddle and both of them going like the wind.

We also had a Jewish boy named Korotkin, who'd been a trick rider in a circus, and one from Warsaw, who was the regiment's champion sharpshooter and partly responsible for our company's regularly winning the regimental championship—until, over a new officer who instantly became known to us as "Haman," we went on strike. But that's another story.

For some reason, even these good Jewish ruffians were awed by our Litvaks. It was as though they realized that *their* martial skills, after all, also were attainable by gentiles, whereas the Litvaks were possessed of something which belonged to us alone.

And so, after all my parents' anxieties that I not be coarsened and corrupted, it turned out that my greatest obstacle to full acceptance by my fellow soldiers was not that I lacked skill with a horse or a rifle—but that I hadn't a firm enough grounding in the Talmud.

13. The Fall (and Resurrection) of Haman

Being only a captain, and in command of a mere company of infantry, Prince Mikhailoff might not have been quite as close a relative to the Czar as he liked to let on. But during the time he was in charge of our company, I must admit I found military life a great deal more interesting and easier to take than the freedom of working a twenty-hour day in Warsaw.

Of course, while we were well aware of our good fortune in having such a humane and easygoing company commander, we naturally continued, among ourselves, to talk as much as ever of the necessity to overthrow our abominable Czar and to abolish altogether such instruments of tyranny as the army. This revolutionary fervor, at least among the Jewish soldiers, was of course still further inflamed as we heard about ongoing pogroms in even such large modern cities as Kishinev and Gomel, and about the latest atrocities committed by the "Black Hundreds," often led by uniformed Russian or Ukrainian officers.

Our noble Mikhailoff was a man who not only enjoyed life, but also did not begrudge others. He believed, for example, that in peacetime there's little sense in tormenting your men with a lot of useless exercises. So, while the other companies were sent on field maneuvers and forced marches and entertainments of that sort, our excellent captain took us, the Fourteenth Company, to some shady spot in the woods. Here he permitted us to amuse ourselves with such leisure activities as trick riding and marksmanship. And we, in anticipation of the revolution, and thanks to Mikhailoff's generosity with ammunition, soon became so handy with our rifles and horses, we began routinely to win a good many of those regimental competitions on whose outcomes our officers so loved to place wagers.

In fact, we did our Captain Mikhailoff so proud, he was presently relieved of his command, promoted to colonel, and placed in charge of an important customs post on the Manchurian border, where it was understood that a man would have to be made of stone not to pile up money like manure.

Very well. We'd had a sensible and humane officer and, instead of simply thanking our good fortune, we'd gone right on plotting the overthrow of his wretched relative, Nicolai Alexandrovich. Now fate rewarded us for our zeal in wanting to liberate our 130 million other countrymen as well.

On a cold Wednesday morning, our new commanding officer made his appearance. He was quite unnaturally tall, with shoulders like a barn door, upon which rested a small Slavic head with a broad nose and little pig eyes. In fact, *all* the parts of his body seemed to be not quite in proportion, so that when he walked, he looked not so much like a man as the way you might picture the original *golem.*

We were promptly called into formation where, for a start, we were allowed to shiver at attention for some time. Presently, our new boss unbended sufficiently to come out and introduce himself as Captain Something-or-other. But before the day was out, his only name among the Jewish soldiers was Haman. Not only because one of his first official acts was to deny some thirty-five of us permission to attend the reading of the Scroll of Esther on the morning of Purim, but, already at this first formation, before he even knew one face from the other, he delivered a speech in which he let us know he was quite well aware that the Fourteenth Company, under its previous commander, had become disgracefully lax, undisciplined, unsoldierly—in short, a virtual vacation resort.

Well, he was here to put an end to all that. Those of us who had forgotten they were soldiers whose bodies and souls belong to the Czar would very quickly find themselves "vacationing" in Siberia. There, before long, they might get the chance to do some *real* soldiering against a race of yellow vermin laboring under the illusion that Asia belonged to *them*. And in particular he advised the Jews in his company to cease conducting themselves as though they were still in some synagogue of theirs.

This final observation, I must say, did not go down too well with the boys in my platoon. Partly thanks to Mikhailoff's easygoing policies, our company, as it happened, had walked away the previous summer, and the summer before that, with the highest score in the Novocherkassky's annual marksmanship competition. Not only because we'd had so much more opportunity to practice, but because, unlike some other companies, we had truly wanted to make a good showing on our captain's behalf. And since a fair number of the Jewish soldiers also happened to be among the best shots in the regiment, it seemed to us that this new *katzap* was starting off with some degree of prejudice.

We had, of course, long been hearing talk about the inevitable war with Japan, and our company's five-man revolutionary committee, of which I was a member, was well aware that if the revolution was put off much longer, we might all soon find ourselves fighting for the Czar's honor in a far-distant Chinese province called Manchuria, where we had as little business to be as the Japanese had being in Korea.

Our committee, therefore, took it as a direct challenge that, at a time when czarism itself, with its incurably corrupt, brutal, and ignorant bureaucracy and army, already seemed on the verge of crumbling, this Haman should come along and try to give *us*, as they say, a taste of pepper.

In short, we determined to settle this dog before he could settle us.

Now, of the seventeen companies in our regiment, ours had long been known as the most militant. This was not due to the leniency of our previous commander, but to the fact that, aside from its high proportion of hard-boiled Litvaks and other such exotic species, our company also boasted a good number of wild and independent tribesmen from the mountains of the Caucasus, including some Gruziyan (Georgian) Jews whose age-old custom it had been to go armed at all times.

One of these crazy Georgians had already made up his mind that Haman had insulted the Jewish nation, and that, as in Georgia, such an insult could be expunged only in blood. In fact, he told none of us what he intended to do, and we found out by sheer accident and barely managed to stop him from putting away Haman right at the outset.

Our new commander, however, got wind of this plot against his life, but unable, despite the most bloodcurdling threats, to find out which man had meant to kill him, he took it out on the entire Fourteenth Company.

Not only did he begin to put us through the kind of training schedule ordinarily imposed only on the so-called convicts' company, but he also let it be known that he was not afraid of us, singly or all together. In fact, he boasted that he had been transferred back here from Siberia, where he'd been perfectly happy, only because he had killed two men who'd made some threatening remarks to him. And he sincerely hoped we didn't think he would hesitate for one moment to do the same thing again, if he had to. After all, the worst that could happen to him would merely be a transfer back to his beloved Siberia.

As a result of this little lecture, it was we who felt obliged now to eat and sleep with our rifles close at hand, in case Haman should decide one night he knew who the ringleaders were.

Not that we intended to sit back and wait for him to play the first card. But, since we were told the time was not yet ripe for open mutiny, we were obliged to find other little ways to let him know we were not exactly paralyzed with fear.

For example, Haman, a rabid stickler for spit and polish, kept a book in which he wrote down all such crimes as unshined boots, loose buttons, or a dirty rifle. If a soldier had enough of these marks against his name, it usually meant a spell in solitary. So, for a start, with the help of a locksmith from Kiev, we broke into Haman's office one night and carefully set fire to his desk, which destroyed not only our book of recorded sins, but a good deal else besides.

Haman raged and threatened, but was unable to discover the "Judas" who had done this to him. So he paid us all back by having us awakened every night for an hour of running around the parade ground while he went peacefully back to sleep.

Fortunately, before he had time to wear us down completely, we remembered that on certain days a group of high officers visited the various mess halls to check on the food. Not so much out of concern for its quality, I suspected, as simply to see that not *too* many of our allotted provisions were stolen by the kitchen personnel and whichever officers were in collusion with them.

So, at the next inspection, by prearrangement, none of us touched the boiled cabbage, which was our main course. And when the inspectors asked us what was wrong with it, we told them nothing was wrong with it, it was just about as good as usual. In consequence, the commission noted down in their book that the Fourteenth Company was given food they couldn't eat.

And while, in Fonya's army, this was surely no crime, our remarkable unanimity did make an impression, and the incident seemed to raise some questions about Haman's managerial talents.

He repaid us promptly the very next morning by having us awakened two hours earlier than usual and put through a succession of calisthenics and bayonet charges which, frankly, left us with very little appetite for breakfast altogether.

It was now clear, of course, to even the dullest of us that when you're dealing with a truly dedicated villain like Haman, these pleasant little pranks would always end up doing us more harm than him. Before he ground us into the dust altogether, we decided we'd better give some thought to how we could rid ourselves of this affliction once and for all.

However, the majority (myself included) very nobly decreed that, for the moment, we were still obliged to draw the line at outright assassination—much to the disappointment of our Gruziyan comrade.

While we awaited the proper opportunity to strike back, Heaven helped, and the despised Japanese attacked and crippled our navy at Port Arthur. Our Little Father who, I suspected, had been praying devoutly for the enemy to do him just such a favor, quickly declared war, confident that the resulting upsurge of patriotic fervor would take people's minds off all such nonsense as revolution. (Not that our *Batyushka Tsar* truly hated the Japanese, whom he only called "monkeys"; his real venom, as we knew, was reserved for the English, whom he called "yids.")

In the days that followed, we learned about the enemy we were about to fight. That is, we were shown pictures that emphasized his smallness and his brutish simian features. It was, in fact, surprising to realize that such a scarcely human creature actually had hands like us, capable of firing a modern rifle, and not mere paws suitable only for swinging from trees.

For now, all the regiments being shipped to Manchuria were under-strength, half-trained, and not even fully equipped. After all, the job of driving these overbearing little creatures back into the sea was not sufficient reason for a great power like Russia to exert its full might.

Meanwhile, our newspapers and officers regaled us with such golden good news, all Petersburg became infected with war fever, any thought of revolution went out the window, and even I found myself caught up in the general excitement. Refusing to listen to my older brother Mordechai, I longed only to be sent to the front and to earn my share of adventures and medals before it was all over and I was obliged to return to Vishogrod and put the humdrum remainder of my life into some matchmaker's hands.

It happened that Haman got wind of my appetite for glory and, with great friendliness, called me into his office and asked if I would like to be sent to Manchuria as a replacement.

Since it was obvious even to me that Haman was not making me this offer out of kindness alone, I backtracked a little and told him that, all things considered, I would prefer to go with my own regiment.

At which he smiled and allowed that he'd long had his eye on me; oh, yes, he knew I was the ringleader of all this scum who'd been plotting mutinies and even assassination against him, and he was delighted now to have this opportunity to be rid of me once and for all.

Fortunately, before my travel orders came through, one of my Ukrainian comrades made a somewhat unnecessary remark about Jews lacking the proper warlike spirit, and by the time they pried us apart, he was bleeding admirably from the head, and I had deep and painful teeth marks in my right hand, which of course I couldn't take to the hospital because they would have wanted to know how I acquired them.

As a result, the day before I was due to board the train to Manchuria, my hand was swollen like a sausage. I could barely pick up a rifle, let alone fire it. The general in charge of medical services decreed that I should remain in Petersburg, so that when the hand had to be amputated, it could be done under the best conditions.

Meanwhile, summer was approaching and, with it, our annual regimental marksmanship competitions. My hand, thanks to the fact that I'd been afraid to go back to the hospital for treatments, was completely back to normal. And Haman, for the moment, had other things than me to worry about.

Each company commander, you must understand, was desperately anxious for his men to make a good showing. These contests, in fact, were one of the few ways in which an officer in garrison could make a name for himself. That was because if a company did really well, its commanding officer got the sole credit, and if it did badly, that, too, was blamed on him. Since there was just about nothing in it for the winning marksmen themselves, these annual competitions, as far as the soldiers were concerned, had only one practical purpose: to demonstrate to the world how the men felt about their company commander.

We could all tell Haman was a little bit worried because for some weeks now, he had been handling us as gently as a mother putting a dressing over an abcess. All our time in the field was devoted totally to marksmanship (although only with the rifle, not the machine gun, which was still too much of a novelty, as well as wasteful of ammunition; also, I think our officers didn't quite trust its reliability—especially in the hands of future revolutionaries).

Haman, of course, already knew that our company was blessed with some of the most expert sharpshooters in the regiment, and he was determined for us to do him proud. We, for our part, had every intention in the world of burying him.

Since Russian infantry tactics had changed very little from the days when soldiers carried muskets and fired in volleys, the way these competitions worked was as follows. Ten men at a time went up to the firing line. A hundred yards away were ten wooden targets painted to resemble enemy soldiers. After each man had fired his allotted number of bullets, a cease-fire was called and some soldiers who'd been hidden in trenches behind the target signaled each man's score with a red flag.

We all knew that, based on past performance, our regimental commander expected the Fourteenth Company to walk away with the first prize, and had placed his bets accordingly. So the night before, our revolutionary committee voted that tomorrow not one of us, all day, was to dare hit his target even once. Somebody wondered whether this wouldn't be a little too obvious. But of course we *wanted* it to be obvious.

Came morning and we took up our positions, fired off our volleys, and with a good deal of careful concentration succeeded in leaving every one of our targets absolutely untouched. I could tell how deeply this pained some of our better marksmen, and how they tried to console themselves by neatly shooting off branches four times as far away as the target.

I glanced over my shoulder and saw Haman's face white as chalk and his teeth biting furiously into his lips. Before long, the colonel, faced with the loss of a rather large bet, summoned him over and, in front of all the visiting dignitaries, raked Haman over the coals for having inspired such blatant disloyalty in his men.

However, we, too, were warned. The results of the first round were declared null and void, and every company was given a fresh chance. Haman watched us in silence, but there was murder in his eye. Nevertheless, once again not one of us inflicted so much as a scratch on a single target.

The colonel, now clearly aware of what sort of a mutiny he had on his hands, also voided the results of the second round, and announced that the contest would continue, all day and all night if necessary, until "certain elements" showed themselves prepared to act like true children of the Czar.

We remained unmoved. By nine in the evening, our company's score still stood at zero, and the other companies, too, had long ceased to take the whole business seriously. The colonel, with barely restrained rage, again nullified all scores, but called a break until the following morning, when the contest would begin afresh.

An hour or two later, the door to our barracks flew open, and Haman entered, alone. We leaped to attention. He told us, in a gentle, almost broken voice, to stand at ease and gather around him.

And he said, "Dear children, I fully understand your grievances against me. I know that, on more than one occasion, I have allowed my vile temper to get the upper hand. And for this now all of you, to a man, are determined to humiliate me. But what am I to do? This is my nature. I've treated my own children no better than I've treated you. All I can do is beg you to forgive my past misdeeds. And let you know that, if you will not help me tomorrow, I am ruined. They will not even send me to an honorable death at the fighting front, but will reduce me in rank and discharge me from the service. And if that happens, there is nothing left for me to do but drown myself or put a bullet through my head."

We listened, but I for one couldn't say I felt particularly moved. Not only didn't I believe what he said, but it seemed to me that if he did kill himself, the world would be well able to survive the loss.

That, however, was not the end of it. Haman now started telling us how his father, an Orthodox priest, had always taught him that Jews were true children of mercy. And he assured us that everyone knew we were the best marksmen in the regiment, and if we were to use our influence on the other men, or even merely do *our* best at the range tomorrow, he would know how to show his gratitude.

His small pig eyes actually erupted with tears. Truly, if a type like this could be reduced to weeping in front of men whom only last week he'd still been calling *zhydovska morda,* the days of the Messiah were at hand.

Haman left, and our little revolutionary cell convened a meeting. All night long we heatedly disputed whether or not to call off our strike.

I argued that, if the man had repented sincerely, he deserved at least one more chance. After all, we had already demonstrated our revolutionary power. Also, if we overthrew Haman completely, what guarantee did we have that our next commander wouldn't be even worse? But there were others who felt that his tears were not sincere, and that we'd be fools to pass up this opportunity to rid ourselves of the bastard once and for all.

In the end, the meeting dissolved without a clear-cut decision one way or the other.

Thus, back at the firing range next morning, some of us

carefully continued to miss our targets, while others ran up a very decent score.

The outcome was still no great triumph for Haman. He was threatened with instant demotion if such a "mutiny" should ever again occur among his men. But he kept his command, and I regret to tell you that his heartbreaking conversion lasted only as long as yesterday's snow.

However, if Haman remained as much of a swine as ever, our little exercise did have one effect. From that day on, our commander's malevolence was strictly impartial. And what Jew in Fonya's army could have asked for more than that?

14. A Blow Struck for the Revolution

On a frosty summer morning, we lined up for the train to Manchuria. Our lieutenant, a moody graybeard in his sixties, who ascribed his low rank to lack of "protection" at court, told us we were lucky. How were we lucky? We would get to ride to the battlefield in comfort, while the enemy, primitive little beasts that they were, would have to walk. He made The Battlefield sound like a scheduled stop on the Trans-Siberian Railway. As for the "primitive" Japanese, I was inclined to suspect they would not exactly receive us with open arms.

My friend Glasnik whispered I should let the lieutenant know we would also be happy to walk, and with a little luck the war would be over by the time we got there. But I was a one-striper, a squad leader, and I kept my mouth shut, scowling with authority.

The train had ninety-six cars, each packed to at least three times what it could hold. This way the railroad was able, on one track, to deliver its quota of thirty thousand replacements a month. I tried not to think about the men we were replacing.

We sat in our compartments, barely able to stir an elbow, each of us still hoarding his own fears and memories. For the moment, Russians, Ukrainians, Poles, and Jews sat packed together in a pleasant atmosphere of revolutionary harmony. That is, somebody started out by wondering how many of us would return alive, and soon somebody else ended up proposing that, at the next halt, we surround our officers and kill them all, then make the train go back to Petersburg and proclaim the revolution.

No one bothered to remember that the officers had all our ammunition under lock and key. Not that it made much difference. They were fine talkers and dreamers, our Russians, but hopelessly addicted to authority. When Glasnik, as usual, wanted to add his comments, I quietly shut him up. I knew from past experience, no matter which way the conversation turned out, they'd end up blaming it all on the Jews.

Days passed. We were all stiff and irritable from the lack of space, and no one talked revolution any longer because by now we hated the stink of one another.

But soon we came to appreciate our crowded compartments. The train had to cross Lake Baikal on rails laid over the ice, which at times suddenly cracked open into yawning rifts and crevices. To keep the cars from being too heavy, the officers were taken across by horse-drawn sledges, and the rest of us walked, our rifles with their eternally fixed bayonets resting on one shoulder. Forty miles across the windswept ice, with only brief pauses for hot soup from our mobile kitchens. By morning it turned out that a number of men had disappeared, probably drowned, and many more suffered from frostbite.

Another week in the unheated train, and one morning we awakened to a strange landscape in which the roofs of the houses curved upward like boats, and the trees put me in mind of things that might be growing on the moon. This was Asia. The people here had darker skins and narrow, villainous, Oriental eyes. Most of the men believed them to be "Japs," having little notion that Japan was almost as far from here as Moscow.

The Orientals scattered like chickens whenever the train came to a halt and we piled out to stretch our legs. Only some peddlers were willing to approach. The officers drove them away, thinking they might be spies.

At one of our stops we were told to send a detail to a nearby village. They were to fetch five oxen purchased for us to slaughter for food. After a week on little but hard black bread, foul soup, and hot tea, we awaited their return in high spirits. Suddenly, commotion. Three of our five men came running out of the woods as though pursued by a demon. They reported how, passing through a lonely stretch of forest, they were set upon by armed "Japs" who tried to steal our oxen.

We ran into the woods with bayonets poised. The oxen were there, unharmed. Nearby, the other two men were lying in a pool of their own blood. One was dead of a knife wound, and the other was still twitching, trying vainly with his hands to stop the spurts of blood.

Someone grimly said, "Well, the war has started." We ran in search of the killers. Deep in the forest we came upon a group of frightened Asiatic civilians who tried to hide from us. Our ranking noncom decided that two of the "Japs" must be killed in retaliation for our men. Since we still had no bullets, we were obliged to use our bayonets.

Some friends and I disgustedly headed back toward the train. Behind us, we heard a couple of screams, then silence, then a burst of loud wailing. It turned out later that the actual bandits were "Chunchus" ("Red Beards"), Chinese brigands who were so powerful and so well organized they didn't hesitate to attack and rob even armed Russian patrols.

Back on the train, gorged with meat, we heard we were headed straight for the battlefield, somewhere between Mukden and Port Arthur, where heavy fighting was taking place. We were said to have lost over sixty thousand men in one battle alone.

Officers came through the cars now to deliver inspirational

talks. About how our Little Father the Czar was counting on each one of us. But mainly about the enemy's cruelty to Russian prisoners. This was to inflame our thirst for blood. In actuality, it had the opposite effect. Most of us were left subdued and depressed. Who wanted to get involved with such uncivilized savages?

Even the Ukrainians and Poles were no longer voicing much eagerness for bloodshed. It was strange to see them so earnest. I wondered if I hadn't misjudged them: if, in past years, it wasn't really we Jews who were guilty of provoking them to violence purely by our insolent helplessness.

Even one of the officers was overheard to remark, "I thought surely by the time we got here the war would be over."

Another young lieutenant, deep in self-pity, observed, "How can they expect an educated man to go and expose himself to being killed or crippled for life?"

The common soldiers once again lapsed into talk of revolution. But in truth, we all knew we were in for it now, and there was no way back except in some condition we'd rather not think about.

Next day our train lumbered to a halt near a village used as a transfer point for the wounded. I could hear no sound of guns yet, but our commandant said we were very close to the battlefield.

Hearts beat more quickly as we were marched through the village. Its principal building served as a field dressing station, and the streets were full of haggard men in Red Cross armbands wearing smeared butchers' aprons. The huts, wherever you looked, were filled with men groaning, gasping, or horribly still. Some of them also lay on the ground outside, listlessly waiting to die. We tried to ask the wounded what it was like, back there. They looked at us blankly.

Later I ran into a Jewish artilleryman I'd known in Petersburg. He had lost one arm, but insisted it was the luckiest thing that ever happened to him. What he told me about the fighting was enough to make your hair stand up. I'd never realized how totally unprepared we were for this war. Unlike the Japanese, we had almost no mountain artillery, nothing but heavy stuff, useless for mobile warfare.

I asked why the wounded weren't taken to hospitals. Answer: because there were none, at least in this sector. The fact was, our high command had expected to engage the enemy much farther to the east, near the Yalu River. But the Japanese had treacherously refused to cooperate.

There was a hospital train on the way. But it was due several days ago and seemed to have disappeared.

A couple of idle and oppressive days among the piteous cries and foul smell of the injured and dying left most of us ready to pray for a quick death rather than the slow one of a serious wound. Then it turned out that our commandant had read his map incorrectly, and stopped the train in the wrong place. The fighting, at present, was said to be at least another half-day's journey from here.

They packed us back into the train, and all ninety-six cars continued on their blind search for the war. But we still didn't reach our destination. This time because the Japanese had blown up a bridge about ten minutes before we got there. They must have had spies all along the line. We were saved only because God is good and our train, as usual, was late.

The adjutant cabled a message to Harbin for engineers and materials to repair the bridge. He was told in turn that we were needed urgently at the front, and he should find boats and ferry us across, then force-march us the rest of the way, some hundreds of miles, with no mention of food.

Fortunately, none of the boats we were able to commandeer was big enough to carry our field pieces, ammunition, or horses, and our commandant, bless him, refused to send us into combat empty-handed.

We soldiers, of course, were quite content to stay right here, and wouldn't have cared if they never fixed the tracks. Except that another troop train now arrived, and suddenly there were thousands of us stranded with barely enough food for a day or two.

Being on a single-track line, with no nearby spurs for detours, we couldn't even send the second train back to get us food. Meanwhile, more trains would be arriving daily, all filled with hungry men.

We were given ammunition for our rifles and told we had to live off the land. The Russian soldier, with his peasant background, is of course a natural-born forager. But in this rocky, frozen soil nothing edible had been growing for the last hundred miles. In fact, the only cultivated fields we'd seen all day were of poppies, grown for the Chinese opium trade.

Some men formed hunting parties. They were warned not to go too far afield. This area was also notorious for bands of the same Chunchus who had killed two of our men some days earlier.

The hunters returned at nightfall with the carcasses of some wild, bushy-tailed cats, a mountain wolf, and several large birds which looked like hawks or buzzards. Hungry as I was, I didn't share in the feast. Even roasted the meat smelled rank, and I could not get myself to eat something when I didn't know what it was.

A day or two later, there was more bad news. Thirty miles behind us, a train carrying food had been blown up by the Japanese. None of *us* had known it was coming, but *they* did. Now we began really to feel trapped, surrounded by invisible spies, and full of heartfelt resentment against such a treacherous enemy.

Meanwhile an engineer had arrived and told the adjutant that the bridge couldn't be repaired. A bypass would have to be built on pontoons, farther downstream. Although no building materials had arrived yet, and the tracks behind us now were torn up as well, we were assured that the job would be done in two weeks. All that without the use of coolie labor, since of course there was no telling who was a spy. (Although Japan and China had been at war only ten years before, we took for granted—correctly, I think—that all Asiatics would stick together against us.)

Not a man believed we would be out of there in less than two to three months. Clearly, by now even the most patriotic Russian blockhead knew that in Fonya's army nothing ever went in a straight line.

Soon there wasn't even a piece of stale brown bread left to distribute. Several men had already died of actual starvation or related diseases. One of them was a boy I was asked to give a Jewish burial. But no one knew his Jewish name to inscribe on the wooden marker over his grave. We settled, for some reason, on "Velvel, son of Avrohom."

Afterwards we tried to sleep, in order to forget our hunger. But not even the gravediggers had the strength to get tired enough. An officer came by and tried to console us. War demands sacrifice. The officers were as starved as we were. If anyone believed him, he kept it to himself.

Glasnik, who was not at the funeral, suddenly returned in great excitement. He had scaled the top of a nearby hill and spotted smoke from the chimney of a house deep in the woods. No telling who lived there, of course. It might even be occupied by an enemy patrol. But hope revived us. A house meant there must be food. That was worth any risk.

But when it came to going to investigate, few of my friends felt strong or adventurous enough. Among the five men who ended up ready to go, I was obliged to include two Russians, one of them a notorious rapist, which I don't suppose made much difference in this case.

By now it was beginning to get dark. Some of the men feared we might get lost and fall into enemy hands. (It wasn't till after the war that I learned that the Japanese, by and large, treated their prisoners quite decently, possibly owing to their ambition to live up to Western standards.)

Rather than postpone our venture until morning, when we'd have to share whatever we found with hundreds of others, I proposed that we go now but take along a machine gun. This, to us, was still a novel and exciting piece of equipment, and we had always envied those who got the privilege of firing it.

But the sergeant in charge of the machine guns knew we were on to something, and wouldn't let us have one unless we promised him an equal share of anything we found. I offered to let him come with us. But, like a good capitalist, he wanted his profit without having to work for it. We made the deal. But just as we were about to wheel out the gun, an officer turned up and wanted to know what was going on. We were forced to make him a partner as well.

Lugging our heavy rapid-fire Maxim gun on its wooden wheels, we pushed our way into the tangled forest. Whatever glimpses we got of the sky didn't give us enough light even to see the noses on our faces. By midnight, it was plain we'd been going in a circle. There was a short, violent quarrel, then we got our bearings once more and continued on. At a quarter past one, I spotted a faint glow in the distance.

Now it belatedly occurred to me: Who would live so deep in the woods except the very bandits we'd been warned about? In a sudden ambush, our machine gun would be worthless. We loaded our rifles and held them at hip level, ready to fire, and tried to proceed as quietly as we could, although our bayonets kept getting caught in the underbrush. But the longer we walked toward the light, the farther off it seemed. Glasnik wondered if we were being lured into a trap.

I told him not to be ridiculous, what did we have that even the poorest bandit would be interested in stealing?

Glasnik pointed to the machine gun.

And how did we know they were merely bandits and not Japanese?

But we had gone too far to turn back now. Just before three o'clock we got our first look at the actual house, a small, primitive stone cottage with a thatched roof. We quietly set up the machine gun at the edge of the clearing, where it could cover the house and all approaches to it.

I volunteered to go ahead and investigate. The house was silent. The chimney was cold, and the light in the window was so pale it might have been only a reflection of the moon. But inside a kerosene lamp was faintly burning, and I could see a broken stove, a pair of high boots which seemed stained with blood, and two ancient rifles hanging on the wall.

I signaled to the others. Two more joined me. Together we burst through the door, our rifles poised to fire. A scrawny, Asiatic woman whose age I found impossible to guess lay snoring on one of the straw mattresses. She didn't stir at our entrance. We searched the room and were delighted to find two bottles of good vodka. Better yet, we opened a trunk and found a large loaf of white bread. The two men left with the machine gun heard us exclaim and came running to join us. There was nearly a fight over dividing the bread. Within moments not a crumb of it remained.

While I tried to restore order, the rapist saw the old woman. He was apparently so starved for female companionship, he tore the cover off the bed, and, in a typical display of Russian finesse, he threw himself on top of her. She awakened with a scream, dodged under his arm, and lunged for the knife we used for cutting the bread. Then she saw us and dropped the knife, crossed herself, and begged for mercy. I assured her we'd come only for food. She glanced at the rapist and was convinced I was lying. But she gave us a pot of sour milk and went looking for other food she could let us have.

It seemed to me she was searching the house as though she were a stranger here too. But she was probably in a state of shock and forgot where she put things. To help calm her down, I sent the rapist out to guard the machine gun.

Minutes later, he saw her hobbling by outside with another pot of sour milk and, crazed with passion, he charged at her once more.

The old woman shrieked like a goat, the sour milk spilled, and we all piled on, trying to separate them. After a wild scramble, I got up covered with sour milk and somebody's blood. The rapist apologized. He said he couldn't understand what came over him.

We continued to search for food. Deep inside the stove, I found a pan of something that looked like blintzes. We stuffed it all into a stocking made of some blanketlike material.

Now, ready to leave, we decided also to take the rifles hanging on the wall. But the woman started to plead with us, half in gestures, half in Russian. They'd kill her if the rifles were gone. "They"? Who were "they"? Her babbling grew so incoherent, the devil only knew what she was talking about.

But I still didn't like to leave rifles where someone could use them to shoot us in the back. We reached for the weapons to make sure that at least they were unloaded. The old woman started to scream again, and suddenly dropped to the floor like a stone.

Abruptly sobered and ashamed of ourselves, we packed up to get out of there. It was nearly four in the morning. We assumed that whoever "they" were they would bury the old woman if she was dead.

As we started to leave, I found Glasnik had decided to search the chicken coop. Now, in a shaken voice, he called me over.

Inside, my foot stumbled against something soft on the floor. I struck a match, and we were overcome with horror. Here lay the murdered bodies of a man and a woman, obviously the real owners of this place. He, with the hard hands and stocky build of a woodcutter, had been killed with his own ax.

No wonder the old woman had searched for food as though she didn't know her way around. Her accomplices, then, to whom the rifles belonged, could not be far away.

The rapist was the most indignant. While we were discussing what to do, he went around acting as though *he*'d suspected the old woman all along. If only we hadn't interfered, he would already have found out everything.

It was near dawn, and we were dead tired. But the majority voted to set up an ambush with the machine gun. None of us had ever fired at a human target. I think that must have been part of the attraction. When the bandits returned, we would avenge their crimes.

My belly had a pleasant glow of bread and vodka. Yet the whole incident had left a bad taste in my mouth. Perhaps it is true that war turns men into beasts. But I would have preferred for us to start back and leave the punishing to God. We, after all, had stolen too, and perhaps murdered as well. But the two Russians were dying to use the new machine gun.

At daybreak, we were barely able to see straight any longer, and still no sign of the bandits. Maybe they knew we were there. By eight o'clock we were ready to give up, when we saw nearly a dozen men approach in single file, two of them carrying a quantity of chickens between them on a pole. A fierce and dissolute-looking bunch, armed with rifles, axes, knives. I looked at them and knew I would have hated to meet them in an open fight.

How glad I was now that we had the machine gun. The bandits cautiously approached the hut. The rapist had his finger curled around the trigger, panting with eagerness to fire a burst. But how did I know for certain these were bandits and not merely woodcutters? Had I the right to judge them by their appearance alone? I motioned to the rapist to wait another moment. This proved to be a bitter mistake, because there was suddenly a cry of warning. The old woman we had left for dead stood in the door of the hut, waving her arms, shouting.

While I stared at her in astonishment, and the rapist foolishly still waited for my signal, the bandits, quick as mice, scattered for cover. Within seconds, they were deployed, crouched behind trees, their rifles searching for targets. That's what I got for being slow to shed blood. Now even if we'd wanted to leave them in peace, it was too late.

I signaled the rapist. He, instead of traversing, fired a long wild burst at the middle of the group. Even so, our opening volley seemed to kill or wound nearly half of them. The others, with incredible speed, vanished back into the woods. The old woman, too, had disappeared. One of their wounded was screaming. The rapist wanted to keep on firing, but the gun already had overheated. Across the clearing, the chickens on their pole lay in plain sight. But none of us dared to go fetch them.

We packed up and started running. The heavy wheeled machine gun slowed us down, but, being personally responsible, I refused to let it be abandoned. We kept looking anxiously behind us, and tried to listen for any sound of pursuit. At the same time, of course, we could not know if they hadn't cut ahead of us and set up an ambush.

But no one interfered with us. Perhaps they took us for a larger unit. We paused just long enough to fill ourselves with water from a spring and to finish every last one of the blintzes. I had some regrets now about leaving the chickens, but at least we'd made sure there was nothing left for the sergeant and the officer, waiting like capitalists for their unearned share. In that small way we felt we had struck a blow for the revolution.

15. The Phantom Synagogue

When you consider that, officially, we had come from the opposite corner of the world for no reason other than to liberate the Chinese empire from Japanese domination, I found it very strange that even the Manchurian coolies our army employed as laborers along the Trans-Siberian Railway all appeared, with some mad sense of Asiatic solidarity, to be spying for the Japanese against *us*, their liberators.

One result of this bizarre loyalty was that the enemy, as I told you, had already done us the kindness of blowing up a bridge only minutes before our train was due to cross it. This, to no one's regret, postponed our arrival on the battlefield by nearly a month, and so, if nothing else, gave many of us four weeks longer to live.

In time, unfortunately, our engineers managed to put up some sort of temporary bridge, which it was best not to examine too closely, and our train resumed its breathless progress toward the theater of war. This time we traveled not only with leaden hearts, knowing we were in for a fight to the death against an enemy who had no appreciation for Europe's civilized traditions of warfare, but also braced, with each jolt of our battered wheels, for another treacherous Asiatic explosion.

At the same time, the half-blind windows of our car offered us only the brutal monotony of barren hills, rotting fields, and mute, hollow-eyed villages. In most places, even the opium poppies lay unharvested.

At last, after the devil knows how many more days of such tourism, we awoke early one morning to find our train pounding into a city we were told was Harbin. A maimed soldier I had met during a halt back in Siberia had told me that Harbin, although technically a Chinese city, had a sizable Russian colony and was in fact known as "the Moscow of the Far East" (largely, it seemed, owing to the capital and enterprise of Siberian Jews). And, although he had not seen it with his own eyes, he also thought there might be some kind of synagogue, established by either Russian or "Cathayan" Jews.

I was relieved to hear this, because I had for some time now been anxiously counting the days, and according to my calculations Kol Nidre night fell on this very evening. Clearly, then, Harbin was the only place in all China where I might yet have a chance to spend Yom Kippur in the midst of a functioning congregation.

It was, on my part, no longer altogether a matter of piety. After hearing some of the returning wounded tell of what went on at the front, I was, simply, not very optimistic about surviving the year to come. This made me doubly determined to be in a place of holiness tonight, where I might plead, for my parents' sake if not my own, to be inscribed and sealed in the Book of Life.

No one of course knew whether our regiment would stay here any length of time or would be sent right on into battle. We knew our lines were crumbling in the face of the Japanese advance, and anything was possible. But I had made up my mind: if there was a synagogue in Harbin, nothing, not even the prospect of standing trial for desertion, would stop me from finding it tonight. (Perhaps I also had a more selfish reason. My younger brother, Avrohom, had been sent to Manchuria a month earlier, and I knew that, if he was still alive, no power on earth would have prevented him from attending.)

At the depot, I picked up the hopeful rumor that we were to spend the next few days at an encampment near the city. "Near" turned out to mean a march of several hours, through a swampy, roadless, thickly wooded wilderness in which not a single landmark offered any assurance I'd be able to find my way back.

As evening approached, I was left with a heavy heart. Our camp was in such a state of disorder that none of the officers even knew about food or tents for the newly arrived regiment. It was obviously futile, amidst all this chaos, to ask for permission to go back to Harbin. Especially for an errand so frivolous as asking the faraway God of the Jews to forgive our sins.

Some of the Jewish soldiers in our regiment had in fact already begun to talk about arranging for services right in camp. However, many of them seemed strangely convinced that Yom Kippur did not begin until the following evening, and there was no way I could convince them otherwise.

Yet even those few who agreed with me felt it was hopeless to try and walk back all the way to Harbin that night. First of all, no one knew the way. Second, although none of us had kept precise track of how many kilometers or how many hours we were from the city, it was felt we could no longer possibly arrive in time for Kol Nidre. Finally, the area we would have had to cover on foot was reported to be swarming with Chinese bandits, who had already killed and robbed and mutilated a number of our stragglers.

For all these reasons, I managed in the end to convince no one but my friend Glasnik that the rumor about bandits was obviously spread by our own officers as the only way to keep us all from wandering off. But the principal thing which persuaded Glasnik was the prospect I painted for him of being invited to a fat, traditional Jewish meal after the fast, and perhaps even of spending this very night in a warm, clean, feather bed.

On Glasnik's insistence, we went first to the tent of our

commanding officer. We found him snoring like an exhausted horse. I politely shook his arm several times, and when that obtained no results, I shouted in his ear. He continued to snore. Finally, in desperation, I lifted him up and dropped him once or twice. But the only response I got was yet another burst of alcoholic fumes. The floor under his cot disclosed two empty vodka bottles. Hopeless.

Glasnik, at this point, felt inclined to give up. What more could the Almighty expect us to do? He suggested waiting at least until we had had a hot meal to help us fast. I told him I was as hungry as he, but that we had a long walk ahead of us, and, with him or without him, I intended to waste not another minute. In the end, Glasnik, purely for friendship's sake, agreed to go along.

We carefully loaded our revolvers and filled our pockets with bullets, and I gave someone my watch, with instructions to send it to my parents in case I was killed en route by the bandits.

It was no work at all to evade the few tired sentries guarding the camp. As darkness fell, we were already well on our way, blundering through a misty landscape strewn with unseen rocks, knee-deep patches of mud, and unexpected rivulets which left our boots filled with water.

I still felt reasonably sure this was the way back to town. But with no visible moon or stars, and no landmarks to guide us, we walked and walked, and Harbin seemed as far away as ever.

Presently, we came upon a narrow road. I had, by this time, no idea in which direction to go. But I reasoned that every road must lead from somewhere to somewhere, and if we only stayed on it, sooner or later we were bound to come to a village in which we could ask directions.

Glasnik, momentarily reassured, suggested we stop for a rest, and we sat down at the base of a tree. Before long, chilled and damp as I was, I began drifting off to sleep and forced myself to get up. I had to shake Glasnik to awaken him. He was fiercely annoyed, and told me to leave him alone. He said it was selfish and stubborn of me to have talked him into going along, when it was perfectly plain to everyone else that Yom Kippur didn't start until tomorrow night. I was able to get him back on his feet only with the cruel threat that, if he fell asleep again, I would leave him, and he would wake up with his throat cut.

After another hour of walking, with no visible progress, Glasnik said that the way he felt right now, anyone who would stab him or shoot him to death would only be doing him a favor. I helped restore his energy by pointing out to him that, from what I'd heard, when these bandits caught a Russian soldier they didn't kill him all at once. They had a method called "the death of a thousand cuts," by which they whittled away at him piecemeal until, after several days, he was fortunate enough to expire.

By now, neither of us had the slightest idea of what time it was. The only thing on which we agreed was that it was long past Kol Nidre. But, if we were going in the right direction, there was still a chance we might find at least a Jewish home where we could get a warm bed and, tomorrow night, a festive meal.

The path now meandered through a dense and dripping forest, in which it was easy to imagine almost any tree giving shelter to some bandit waiting for just such foolish travelers as ourselves. Both of us tried hard to walk without making any noise. But our frequent stumblings made this impossible. The forest seemed endless. I felt more and more tempted to lie down under a tree and go to sleep. The only thing that kept me on my feet was the recollection that that morning we also had passed through a deep wood, and perhaps this road would, at least, lead us back to our camp. Glasnik agreed, and both of us broke into a steady trot, hoping to reach camp undetected, still in time to get some sleep.

But almost the moment we were out of the forest we heard, through the fog-blanketed gloom, the ghostly piping of a voice.

Glasnik seized my arm. I irritably shook him off. But I, too, felt the hair congealing on the back of my neck. To control my momentary panic, I took out my revolver and warned Glasnik to keep his mouth shut.

The sound drifted closer. It was something halfway between the shriek of a demon and the whinny of a horse. Glasnik suggested that, if this was a Japanese patrol, we should kill as many as we could, and then, rather than face being captured and tortured, we should shoot ourselves.

Now, for a time, there was silence again. But we refused to let down our guard. Holding on to each other's belts so that, in the dark, we didn't accidentally shoot one another, we stalked the source of that ghostly, piercing sound.

A dark, broad shape now came floating slowly toward us. We moved aside to let it approach. Presently, it began to appear that the demonic noise was being made by a mule staggering and swaying under its load. Leading it was a stocky, villainous-looking Chinese. We abruptly stepped forward with outthrust revolvers, and saw with satisfaction that he was as terrified of us as we were of him.

"Put up your hands," I commanded him. The Chinese looked at our weapons and promptly understood Russian. But now that his hands were up, I was no longer sure of what to do next. Take him prisoner? How would this help us find a synagogue?

To keep the Chinese from realizing how uncertain I was, I instructed Glasnik to point the gun at the man's head while I searched his cargo, not without a sense of shame, feeling like a highway robber.

But my embarrassment vanished when I saw that aside from apples and tobacco leaves, our prisoner also carried a loaded revolver of the kind worn by Russian cavalrymen. In other words, he was not just a farmer but a bandit, or, at the very least, one of those repulsive creatures who scavenged battlefields and robbed the dead.

The Chinese now stupidly played on my sense of indignation by sinking to his knees and begging for mercy. Clearly a man with a guilty conscience. Only what kind of just punishment was I in a position to mete out, and tonight of all nights, when I myself stood before the divine Seat of Judgment?

But, having gone this far, I didn't quite know how to back-track. So, playing for time, I began to examine the remarkably large bundle being carried by the mule, and suddenly I thought I heard a human moan. I looked at the Chinese. His eyes stared up at me in utter terror. I took a knife and cut open the bundle. A body came bursting out and dropped at my feet. Another Chinese, cruelly bound and gagged. I cut his bonds and for a moment he was unable to stand. But as soon as he had regained his feet, he threw himself down and hugged and kissed my boots. It seemed to me I must have saved him from certain death. Meanwhile, Glasnik, instead of keeping his gun pointed at our mysterious captive, had been eating some of his Chinese apples.

I asked him what *he* thought we should do with this bandit we had captured.

"Well, we can't shoot him," he declared, as though he had given the matter a great deal of thought.

I had, of course, no intention of shooting him, but I demanded to know why Glasnik felt we couldn't if we wanted to.

"What if he belongs to a gang, and they hear the shot?"

I was forced to admit he had a point. "What do we do then, let him go?"

Glasnik shrugged and bit into another apple. I motioned to our captive to get up and start running. He bowed to us and tried to kiss me. I pushed him away. He finally started to run like a man who expected to get a bullet in his back at any moment.

It occurred to me that the man whose life we had saved might be able to tell us how far we were from Harbin, and what would be the shortest way to travel. But when I turned to look for him, I found he, too, had disappeared.

The mule, meanwhile, was nibbling at some stubby grass, and Glasnik had put a wad of tobacco into the pipe he had taken from our captive and was puffing contentedly. "I never thought it would be so easy."

"What?"

"We seem to have a talent for it. Why couldn't we settle

down here and make a living as bandits? Look at how easy it was."

"Sure. The other bandits here will welcome us with open arms."

"What's better? To go back to the regiment and be killed in battle?"

"For now, I'll be satisfied just to find a synagogue."

We had left camp at half past six, and by now it must have been close to midnight (although Glasnik insisted it was already almost morning). But both of us agreed to continue trying to make our way to Harbin. Especially now that we had a mule.

Meanwhile, however, I began to get nervous about the bandit we had released. He knew the area and we didn't. What if he and some of his comrades decided to come after us?

Once more we tried in haste to get the mule away from the grass. Not a hope. Nor did it have a bit in its mouth by which we could pull it. Glasnik finally improvised a halter out of some rope, and we climbed on the mule's back.

The animal chose precisely this place to lift up its head and emit a mulish noise that, I was certain, could be heard for miles. If bandits were waiting to ambush us, the mule was their perfect accomplice.

Glasnik tried to tie up the mule's mouth. But we soon realized that the animal had only been trying to warn us, because, in our insistence that it obey our directions, we had forced it to head straight into a swamp.

Glasnik, who was holding the reins, already was straining to get us back out. I jumped down to help him and promptly sank in up to my hips. And now, as if to tantalize us in the midst of our struggles, the lights of a city appeared to be glowing just beyond the forest.

Fortunately, the swamp was mostly water, and in the end Glasnik and I managed to pull each other back out. The mule, however, had merged with the darkness, and neither of us felt inclined to go looking for it.

Caked with mud and soaking wet, we stumbled on into the

silent city. By the light of a dim street lamp, Glasnik and I regarded each other's inhuman appearance, and decided to look for a pump where we could wash at least our hands and faces.

After blundering through half a dozen streets or alleys, we spied a light burning in a little hut next to a store, and decided to knock on the shutters.

A Chinese man opened the door and gaped. Behind him, a squirming mass of seven or eight children instantly started to cry at the sight of us. The man whispered something to his wife, who promptly shot out the back door, screaming for help.

We kept trying to explain to the man that we only wanted some water to wash off the mud. Other Chinese now came running out of nearby shacks. I realized indignantly that, far from being terrified, they were laughing at us.

I kept asking and gesturing for water. Finally I waved a ruble at them, and within moments, two brimming pails appeared.

One of the Chinese, who seemed to know about a dozen words of Russian, now offered, for a ruble, to act as our guide. He looked at least a hundred years old. But the way I was feeling at this moment, money was no object, if he could only show us the way to the synagogue, which we tried to represent to him, with the aid of all sorts of Hasidic gestures and contortions, as a place of prayer.

His face lit up with sudden understanding. He motioned us to follow him. After some twenty minutes of walking we came upon an old frame building. Candles were burning inside.

Glasnik, with great skepticism, asked me, "You know how to pray in Chinese?" I, too, was somewhat unconvinced. Meanwhile, our guide had gone into a corner to argue or negotiate or plot with the caretaker he had aroused. It was ominously clear to me that they were discussing us. And I can't say I much liked the way they looked in our direction.

So I interrupted our guide in the middle of his earnest conversation and asked him whether there was some kind of inn or hotel anywhere in the vicinity.

Now, all the Chinese I ever met in Manchuria had the same habit. When they didn't understand what you said to them, they would smile and nod reassuringly, while echoing your statement in their own singsong.

Our interpreter suddenly seemed to have forgotten even his modest repertoire of twelve Russian words, and his singsong repetitions of everything I asked him became so musical that Glasnik said it was possible he was the cantor of the synagogue.

But it turned out that the interpreter did have a clear idea of what he wanted to do for us next. Tugging us by the sleeve, and talking with gestures and an occasional Russian word, he managed to convey that he was taking us to a place in which any variety of female favor could be obtained.

Glasnik, I'm sorry to say, seemed ready enough to let himself be forced. But I was angry. I said, "Was it for this that we dragged ourselves through the mud all night, and nearly got killed by bandits?"

"And where else can we stay until morning?"

I said, "Any other time I wouldn't care. But on this sacred day, when a week from now we might be dead, should we throw away our last opportunity to be inscribed for a good year?"

Glasnik began to look abashed.

"Besides," I said, "the man is obviously either a crook or a total incompetent."

"How do you know?"

"If he couldn't find a synagogue, how do you know he'll be able to find the other kind of house? He's probably trying to lure us some place where we'll be killed and robbed."

The Chinese, seeing me get the upper hand, made one more effort by tugging at Glasnik's sleeve. Angry to see my friend weakening once more, I drew my revolver and pointed it at our guide. At this, he finally gave up on us and ran away. Yet Glasnik still refused to admit that I had been right about this man.

We now continued wandering through lanes ankle-deep in mud, looking for the Russian quarter. Before long, Glasnik began to complain to me as passionately as the children of Israel had once murmured against Moses for having taken them away from Pharaoh's fleshpots and made them blunder through the endless desert. The difference was that Moses could at least talk to God, while I couldn't even talk to a Chinaman.

Passing a drab wooden building without windows, we suddenly heard ghostly, disembodied voices, like reverberations from the bottom of a well. We drew closer to the entrance, which consisted of a large, flapping rag, and found our noses assailed by a strange odor.

I told Glasnik this must be a Chinese restaurant. Glasnik sniffed once again and refused to believe that these odors could have anything to do with food for human beings.

I shared his distaste, but I reasoned that a primitive restaurant also might offer some accommodations for the night, and just as they say poverty can break iron, so I supposed that exhaustion can tolerate the smell of Chinese food. We entered cautiously, our hands on our revolvers.

Inside, rows of Chinese were sitting on the bare floor with their feet folded beneath them. A man I assumed to be the owner came out and began to talk at us, presumably asking what we wanted to eat. I tried to explain to him we were looking only for a place to sleep, but Glasnik interrupted, gesturing in a way that would indicate to him we wanted food, lots of it.

The owner smiled, nodded, and went into what, from the smell, I judged to be the kitchen. Glasnik pointed out to me that I had no proof this was Yom Kippur, and was it not a *mitzvah* to eat well before the fast?

"I know what he'll bring you to eat," I told him. "I've heard about these Chinamen. He'll bring you a roasted cat, or a boiled dog, or a pickled snake."

Glasnik had turned green, but bravely insisted that the food could not possibly taste as bad as it smelled.

A waiter finally came out of the kitchen, and set down two bowls in front of us. Glasnik sniffed at his portion and seemed ready to gag. He said, "I want to see you eat first."

I shook my head. Glasnik dug his chopsticks into the bowl and tried to pick up a mouthful. It all fell back. The other Chinese started to laugh. Glasnik promptly put down his chopsticks and commenced eating with his hands. The other customers now were roaring with laughter.

Glasnik suddenly spit out and gagged. But he had accidentally splashed one of the nearby customers, and I saw now that all of them had just been waiting for an opportunity to start a fight with us. They crowded us into a corner. I tried to reach for my revolver, and the owner tried to push himself between us and warn the others we were armed.

I suggested to Glasnik that we leave. He said no, not until he had beaten up the Chinese who had started the fight. But I had seen the flash of knives in the dimly lit room, and convinced Glasnik that some of these people were probably bandits and we'd be lucky just to get out of there alive.

Both of us edged toward the door, holding our revolvers pointed at the crowd.

Outside, a smudged gray sun was lightening the sky. I saw some Russian-looking men at the end of the street, and ran toward them. They took one look at our appearance and started to run away. We had to chase them for several blocks before I could corner them and ask if they knew of a synagogue in this town.

One of the men replied in Yiddish that he didn't know about a synagogue, but there was a Jewish-owned restaurant not far away, and we could inquire there.

Both of us brightened at the thought of a hot Jewish meal after the fast, or even before if, as Glasnik now insisted, I was wrong about the date. We ran in the direction the man had indicated. Some blocks away we found ourselves suddenly enveloped by a bizarre parade. It centered around a man crouched in a narrow bamboo cage, guarded by police, and followed by friends or relatives who uttered shrieks of prayer and shot off religious fireworks. (This, someone explained to me later, was a criminal sentenced to beheading, and the fireworks were to awaken the sleeping gods and prepare them to receive the new soul. Lesser criminals, I learned, were merely disabled by having an arm or a foot chopped off, to save the expense of supporting them in jail.)

The caged criminal suddenly reached out through the bars and nearly succeeded in snatching Glasnik's pipe. I stared at him, dumbfounded. He seemed to me to bear an astonishing resemblance to the very man we had rescued from the bandit the night before. I admit that, to some extent, all Chinese still looked alike to me. Besides, as our lieutenant had explained to us, "There are only two kinds of Chinese—those who give bribes and those who take them." And yet, I wondered, could I stand by while a monstrous injustice seemed about to take place?

Although it was certain to make us late for the synagogue, my first impulse was to follow the cage and try to explain to someone in authority that we knew this fellow, and that, in fact, he himself had suffered at the hands of a bandit. To Glasnik, though, the prisoner looked nothing whatever like the man from the night before. Then I saw that the ragged policemen who accompanied the prisoner were wearing flat straw hats on which their rank was indicated by a piece of glass tied on with red string, just like the "bandit" whose prisoner we had so nobly set free.

I grabbed Glasnik's arm and we ran.

Only a few blocks away, we suddenly came upon a building that was unmistakably a synagogue. We were just in time to see the cantor mount the pulpit and hoarsely announce that he had caught cold, and therefore his prayers would not be up to their usual standard.

When he finally started to sing, I suspected that he would not have done much better without a cold. Still, he was the *shliah tzibur*, the "intermediary of the community," and if the words that came groaning out of his mouth satisfied the Almighty, who was I to complain? Starved, exhausted, and muddy as we were, we had achieved our goal. I was, in fact, beginning to tell myself that all of our hardships of the night before had been worthwhile after all, and that Heaven surely would take note of the trouble to which we had gone, when I felt Glasnik nudging me, guiding my eye.

I looked around me and saw no sign of Avrohom. But there were at least one hundred soldiers here from our regiment. All of them, instead of setting out blindly the night before, had arrived in the morning, just ahead of us, clean, well rested, with a good dinner under their belts, and with proper authorization and even a guide to show them the way. Glasnik gave me a ferocious look. Yet I must say I felt no envy of their neat, unruffled appearance. For when the moment came to cry out to the Almighty that here I stood before Him, crushed and confounded, "having gone astray and led astray," no tears in all Manchuria were more wholehearted than mine.

16. The Lost and Found Battlefield

At Mukden, we heard from soldiers guarding the railroad station that our losses on retreating—or to be accurate, escaping—from Port Arthur had run into the tens of thousands. Thus, our train and its human freight were needed urgently now not only to help fill the gaping holes in what was left of our front lines, but also to evacuate an endless stream of torn and broken men for whom no hospital beds were available locally.

I know from books I've read since then that the war was believed to have been provoked deliberately by the Czar, since he expected to make short work of the primitive little yellow men and their insolent territorial ambitions. But, from what I saw at first hand as we reached Manchuria, the best proof of how little the Russians actually expected a Japanese attack was how totally and nakedly unprepared our army and navy were, both for the fighting and for its natural consequences. (To be fair, I am not certain that, even if our generals had been diligently planning this war day and night for the past ten years, they would have done much better.)

From Mukden, we were obliged to continue on foot. Plainly, at long last, we were headed in earnest for the battlefield, and this time, surely, nothing but a miracle could delay us once again.

But our general, long life to him, proved himself to be just such a miracle. A dried-up, snowy-haired little man, General Z. bravely had relinquished his private railroad car, most of his personal baggage train, all but one of his servants, and a mistress who remained in his car and later was rumored to have been the cause of several duels. Now, late at night, he was riding near the head of our column and, with the aid of a pair of opera glasses mounted on lorgnettes, searched the mutilated landscape for some sign of the inscrutable enemy.

From time to time, he also condescended to rein in his horse so that, by the flicker of a trembling candle, he might consult a large, tattered old map from which, it seemed to me, he extracted as much enlightenment as a chicken studying the commentaries of Rashi.

But if, during our interminable tramp through the icy Manchurian blackness, even our dullest Russian peasants now cursed the army and wished they were home, this was not to say our men were lacking in courage. If you want my opinion, people write a lot of foolishness about the bravery of this or that nation's soldiers. But I say, *all* soldiers are brave. Brave and stupid. If they were not, how would you ever get them near a battlefield in the first place? No army in the world would have enough firing squads to make them go.

If I try now to give you the larger picture in which our regiment's role was no more than an accidental brush-stroke, you must understand that, in all truth, like any other *golem* of a soldier, once the real fighting began, I saw little farther than the tip of my nose. What actually happened around me I only found out when I read about it years later.

The occasion (unless I read the wrong book) was known as the Battle of Liao-Yang, and it involved more men than any battle fought in modern times, including Waterloo. And yet, no one in America ever heard of this battle; which for the sake of Russian honor may be just as well.

To begin with, in our training we had learned nothing whatever about modern advances in infantry tactics, while the despised Japanese, in their shameless eagerness to be westernized, were up on all the latest tricks. Our leaders also were smugly ignorant about the Japanese mentality, their fanaticism, their patriotic fervor, their incredible endurance, their horribly unpredictable methods of attack, or even their weapons and in what way these might stack up against ours.

In fact, it soon was obvious that most of our officers still visualized ground combat in terms of the war they had fought against the Turks thirty years earlier.

Meanwhile, of course—almost behind our backs—the doctrines of infantry combat had been totally overturned several decades earlier by the American invention, or perfection, of the machine gun. Not that our Maxim was not at least as good as the Hotchkiss used by the Japanese. The difference was *they* knew how to employ it with some tactical effectiveness, while to us it was just another burden some poor donkey of a foot soldier had to haul over the frozen ground.

Our repeating rifle, too, was actually superior to those with which the Japanese were armed. Unfortunately, the invention of smokeless powder (about which I suppose no one had bothered to inform our general staff) had also increased the range, accuracy, and penetrating power of rifle bullets, which allowed the Japanese foot soldiers to be armed with a more lightweight rifle and enabled each man to carry twice as many bullets.

Of course, when you consider that we were up against a mentality which was willing, for example, to squander 100,000 lives for the capture of Port Arthur, the Russian infantryman, for all his stubbornness and bravery, was obviously not insane enough to try to outdo his Asiatic enemy. Especially since, at least in our regiment, the majority of the common soldiers were not Russians at all, but Poles, Jews, Ukrainians, Balts, and even Germans, all of whom loved the Czar (as well as their Russian comrades) about as warmly as a chicken loves the fox. And there was yet another good reason why we made such a poor showing. Throughout the army the only force able to stir the average czarist soldier out of his brutish apathy, aside from self-preservation, was talk of revolution.

But, of course, these were all things I fully understood only long afterwards. For now, at the outset of our first night's excursion in search of the battlefield, there was mostly a lot of grumbling about the cold, the lack of food, and, more perfunctorily, about the "Japs" (a term which for us also included Siberians, Manchurians, Koreans, and Chinese). Despite all the "inspirational" talks about Japanese atrocities we'd been given en route, we didn't really hate them as yet. Our purest hatred, born of long-festering national and religious animosities, still was reserved for one another—Pole against Russian against Jew against Ukrainian. . . . The Japanese we merely feared, although not as much as we feared the villainous incompetence of our own junior officers.

At the same time, the Jewish soldier of course knew that, no matter how bravely he did his part, or even offered up his life, if Russia won the war, he would be going home to precisely the same morass of poverty, discrimination, and intermittent pogroms. (I recall, long after the war, seeing a watercolor painting of a one-legged Jewish soldier resting on a crutch as he faced the artist, gaunt-eyed, in his ragged greatcoat. Underneath was a one-word caption in Yiddish: FARVOS?—"For what?")

Even I, as a corporal, frankly found it difficult to work up much enthusiasm. Didn't I know that, for each official enemy in Japanese uniform, I had a far more dedicated enemy at my side, or behind me? Prominent among these, at the time I'm now talking about, was Pyotr, the sheep-faced Ukrainian sergeant, now demoted and under my command, with whom I'd had such a murderous brawl almost as soon as I arrived in Petersburg as a green recruit.

My friend Glasnik, who in the past year had suffered a good deal from Pyotr's untiring malice, frequently warned me that, regardless of how fairly I tried to deal with my men, "this sheepfaced *katzap"* remained determined to settle old scores. And since I now outranked him, he merely was biding his time until the chaos of battle would make it quite impossible to determine precisely who had been killed by whose bullet.

Glasnik vowed, however, to watch over me and, failing that, to avenge me. His concern not only touched me, but also left me uneasy enough to be quite content for our blundering general not to find the battlefield, even if it meant going hungry a while longer.

Unfortunately, General Z.'s aristocratic contempt for geography and terrain maps was, in the end, more than made up for by the accommodating Japanese. Whether out of Oriental courtesy or simple impatience, the enemy presently came looking for *us*.

However, this first night, the Japanese didn't know yet what sort of a treasure they were dealing with, and therefore made no real effort to meet us halfway. Consequently, our unit, after marching for ten hours through a darkness as dense as the ninth plague, simply failed by morning to appear at the appointed place for the battle.

Footsore, some of my men were grumbling audibly. I advised them to shut up and count their blessings. If we had had a commander who knew his business, they would already have been in battle and possibly dead.

So we plodded on past devastated villages and frozen, long-unburied corpses until, at sunrise, our general, perplexed, halted the column and politely asked some blank-faced Manchurian peasants if they could tell him where to find the battlefield.

The peasants glanced open-mouthed at his map, and professed not to know what he was talking about. This ceremony was repeated several more times, while the men started complaining now about having had no hot food for some twenty hours. But the treacherous Japanese remained the devil knows where.

By noon, the men were totally exhausted, but also relieved to know that we had obviously missed the battle, and by our mysterious absence might even have upset the enemy's diabolical strategy.

Presently, we saw a convoy grinding toward us out of the icy morning fog which smothered the ground. Each wagon was piled high with dead or wounded soldiers, some of the latter still capable of moans and shrieks that, to me, seemed scarcely human. This, it turned out, was the unit at whose flank we were to have fought this morning.

None of us said a word. But it was easy to guess what each man was thinking. Here were men full of life just like ourselves, and look at what had happened to them in only a few short days, perhaps only hours. Even the unwounded, who were obliged to walk, looked shriveled, verminous, hunched like beaten dogs, in muddy, torn, and blood-spattered greatcoats, staring through us out of listless, unfocused eyes.

I tried to ask some of them in passing what had happened back there. Only one man bothered to reply. He said his only wish was for the Czar to spend just one night in the trenches as they had done. He would never again in his life declare a war.

Now we passed a file of stretcher-bearers with those wounded whom they still seemed to have some wild hope of saving. The sight of them reminded me of nothing so much as our Polish town butcher returning home in his smeared apron, carrying a sack with a slaughtered calf's head, lungs, and liver for his wife's pot.

Some of the stretcher-bearers glanced at us professionally, as though wondering how heavy *we* would be to carry after the next encounter.

I could hear some of the men wishing they were already wounded and on their way back; at least they would escape something worse. My friend Glasnik, unwilling to open Satan's mouth, merely wondered why the stretcher-bearers had to wait until he was wounded. Why couldn't they take him right now, while he'd be able to appreciate it?

It was not until I recognized one of the walking wounded that it suddenly hit me. This was my younger brother's company! With a beating heart, I fell in beside him and asked about Avrohom.

He made a negative gesture and averted his eyes.

I clawed at the front of his coat. "What happened to my brother?"

He shrugged.

"Is he dead?"

"I don't know."

"*Tell* me."

"Half the company is missing."

"Captured?"

"I don't *know!*"

In the end, all I could get out of him was that he had not actually seen Avrohom's body, but my brother's platoon was the first to be thrown into the attack and hardly a man among them had survived.

I sat on the ground, choked with tears, and refused to go on. In my exhausted and delirious state of mind, I bitterly reflected that if only our imbecile of a general had found the battlefield in time, my brother's platoon might not have been wiped out.

Some of my squad gathered around and tried to console me. But I was most conscious of the one man who stood aloof and grinning. I could see Pyotr had not for a moment abandoned his determination to settle old scores, probably as soon as we got into the tumult of close combat.

My platoon commander rode up and told me not to believe the other soldier. He personally would make inquiries about my brother and, if he was wounded, make it possible for me somehow to go and see him.

I thanked him, but darkly consoled myself with the thought that, after all, it mattered little which one of us was the first to die, when it was plain that eventually we all would end up buried forever in this strange "Japanese" soil.

We suddenly were halted and ordered to start digging trenches. I noticed that our officers had us deployed on the back slope of a hill in such a way that, while we wouldn't see much of an approaching enemy, we would at least be able to run away more easily. It was nice to see how much faith they had in the Russian infantry's ability to stand fast under frontal attack.

The trenches were to be about twenty feet apart and four and a half feet deep. The digging went easily because the ground here was soft and muddy. But, for the same reason, the sides of the trenches kept caving in.

Before sunset, we were summoned together at the foot of the hill, where our commanding general delivered a talk. He was unquestionably a talented orator, at least as measured by his effect on the Russian and Ukrainian boys. He recounted the greatness of Holy Mother Russia, of how we had never lost a war, and of how devoted our Little Father was to the welfare of his people, regardless of their nationality or religion. Therefore, each man, whatever his origins, should consider it an honor to give his life for the Czar. And after the war, things would be different: peasants would receive more land, workers would get higher wages, and even the Jews present here would have the right to own land wherever they wished to live.

Glasnik pointed out to me afterwards that there was one small catch to these wonderful promises: to see them carried out one merely had to get killed first.

But our general had reassurances for skeptics like Glasnik, too. Our enemy, he said, was more monkey than man, so puny and primitive and so laughably unaccustomed to modern warfare or true Russian patriotic fervor, that to send him into headlong flight we needed to do scarcely more than throw our caps into the air. I thought of the men who had passed us earlier today, and wondered why *they* hadn't thought of that.

With evening, it grew piercingly cold again. We lined up at our soup wagons. The food did little more than warm our stomachs for a moment. But the real hardship was that we couldn't smoke because our lit matches might reveal our location to the enemy. I suspected, however, that the Japanese knew exactly where we were, probably better than we did.

Presently, we were issued bales of straw to spread between

ourselves and the muddy floor of the trench when we lay down to sleep. Glasnik was dying for a cigarette. I forbade it. Some of the men, including Pyotr, huddled under their coats to light matches. I was forced to forbid that, too, if only because there was some danger the straw might catch fire. I realized of course that some of the men still resented taking orders from a Jew, and if at this moment I were to be openly disobeyed, I would either have to swallow it, be ready to use my fists, or, still worse, have to resort, like any incompetent officer, to drawing my revolver.

I forced myself to stay awake, and no further matches were struck.

By morning, all of us were furiously hungry. But nowhere was there so much as a glimpse of food. What I did see were hundreds of soldiers, roaming around, in defiance of orders, collecting clean snow to boil for tea and to wash themselves.

I ordered my men not to leave the trench, and to take just enough water from their canteens to rinse their mouths and eyes. So we waited and yawned and scratched ourselves, and cursed the bitter cold which knifed right through to our bones.

If only we had had some sort of pot in which to boil snow, just to warm ourselves on the steam. By now the frost was so sharp that if you spit, the glob turned to ice even before it dribbled down your chin. After lying all night on the damp, muddy straw, I now felt my uniform and even my underwear frozen as stiff as though they'd been heavily starched. I jumped around and thrashed my arms to work up some body heat. If the Japanese had attacked at that moment, I'm quite sure I would not have been able to hook a finger around the trigger. I could only hope they were as uncomfortable as we were.

Toward noon, an emaciated ray of sun broke through. Further down the line we heard a shout of joy. The soup wagons had arrived. Wild with eagerness, the men started to dance around in total abandonment. Not a person was still in his trench or at his gun, and I knew if I ordered my squad to get back into our trench, there would be open mutiny.

But, just as we lined up for the soup, altogether without thought for cover or concealment, our uncivilized enemy decided to open up with his heaviest artillery. Before we knew it, we were in the midst of a formidably accurate barrage. I saw horses, wagons, and men flung through the air like toys. All around me, soldiers, torn by shrapnel, were screaming. We rushed back to our trenches, full of hatred for the Japanese. But they were too far away for us to reach with our rifles, and the orders now were not to fire. It might give away our positions!

We were, however, consoled by the promise of an opportunity to make a bayonet charge on the enemy's trenches, as soon as we knew where his main strength was concentrated. Meanwhile, far in back of us, dispatch riders were hurrying in all directions, and our adjutant was telegraphing frantically for counter-battery fire.

(It was explained to us later that the reason our own artillery held back was the thievish practice of some Japanese troops deliberately to make targets of themselves for our big guns. That way, and by carefully combing the impact holes for shell fragments, they were able to determine not only the locations of our batteries, but even their exact caliber.)

Our artillery finally came to life, dropping their first rounds on our own forward positions to help them find their range, like a man urinating into the wind. The shelling, now back and forth, continued sporadically until nightfall, while we cowered, starved and useless, in our trenches. After dark, we received a small ration of hardtack brought in by Cossack horsemen. It just about sustained us for the night.

My platoon commander spent the night in our trench, and I felt relieved temporarily of responsibility.

With our stomachs feeling dry and shriveled, we huddled together and tried to sleep. Each squad had been issued a large straw torch and a bottle of kerosene. If attacked, we were to light the torch, and the unit in back of us would counterattack. That, at least, was the plan.

But the Japanese, as usual, didn't wait for a formal invitation. At two in the morning (according to my diary, on November the 2nd, 1904), while I was dreaming about sitting with a girl friend in an ice cream parlor in Warsaw, someone shook me and yelled, "Brother, get up!" I jumped to my feet and immediately ducked again. Machine guns were raking our position, and bursts of shrapnel squealed over our heads.

Our batteries replied, but stingily and without much visible effect. All around us, once again, we heard the shrieks and moans of the wounded. Somewhere in the darkness, a boy cried out in Polish. I started to climb out, but my lieutenant pulled me back. He said we must save our assistance for the men closer to us. He was a kindly soul, but I could see that, as a Russian, he had no great enthusiasm for helping a Polak. Soon the boy's cries began to fade and then died out entirely.

The shelling grew steadily more intense, as well as more accurate. I didn't see how we could live through this night. I'd never thought combat would be anything but terrible, but I had not expected it to be as frightful as this. Presently, I found myself praying for daylight, although this offered no guarantee that the shelling would stop. My lieutenant suddenly screamed, "Lord, have mercy!" and fell on top of me. Covered with his blood, and unable to support his weight, I grew dizzy and, within a moment, found myself lying pinned to the bottom of the trench.

Glasnik pulled me free and kept shouting in my ear, "Marateck, are you wounded?" I stood up and checked where my uniform was bloody, but it was all the lieutenant's blood.

The wounded man was whimpering, "Mother! Mother!" None of us knew how to tie a bandage that would stop his bleeding. I tried to give him some water, but his mouth was tightly clenched from the pain. I knew if we didn't get him to an aid-station at once, he'd die from loss of blood.

Above us, the bombardment was thicker than before. But four of us decided to risk it. Crawling on our bellies, we dragged our lieutenant toward the rear. After going like this for about an hour, we dropped into an empty trench to catch our breath. I struck a match to see how the lieutenant was doing. The match burned down to my fingers. Our platoon commander was without a head, and probably had been for some time. Two of the soldiers began to cry. The sweat had congealed on our bodies, and we now started to shiver from cold.

I bandaged one of the men who had a bleeding finger. But when I tried to tear off the excess bandage, he screamed. The bloody bandage already had frozen to the wound.

An hour later his hand turned black. We got him to an aid-station right after sunrise, before the other wounded came pouring in. There they amputated his arm.

Returning with some stretcher-bearers to pick up wounded men, we saw that many of them no longer needed assistance. Too weak to keep warm by moving around, they had frozen to death. No doubt, it was just as well. The few doctors we had were able to do little more than have us sort out the dead from the wounded.

The doctors wanted us to stay and help them. But now the aid-station itself came under fire. Glasnik and I decided if we were to die this morning, let it be at the front, with our own squad.

Later, during a letup in the shelling, one of our regimental staff officers came by on horseback and told us we had won a great victory. Despite heavy losses, we had held our position. I was too tired to point out to him that the hill belonged to China, not to us, and that the Japanese infantry had not as yet made an actual effort to take it. Further down the line, a cheer went up as the next platoon was informed of its "victory." I sat on the damp straw and prayed to be spared any more such military triumphs.

In midafternoon, there was a fresh artillery duel, but the enemy had shifted his interest to another sector, and we were able to sleep. Toward evening, I climbed out of the trench to see about the soup. With a shock, I found that all the nearby trenches were empty. Our battalion, it seemed, had been withdrawn while we were asleep. The wind and sleet had covered all tracks, and it was impossible to tell in which direction they had gone. If we tried to look for them, now that it was beginning to get dark, we might walk right into enemy hands.

Here we were then, alone on a huge sloping field, surrounded by the twisted bodies of men and horses, piles of empty ammunition boxes, boots, shovels, mess tins, broken carts, fur hats, blankets, and scraps of clothing. Pyotr, my devoted enemy, had the excellent idea of searching the dead for any hardtack, sugar, or tobacco they might have on them. Soon we were all doing it. We found very little, until we searched the pack of an officer, which yielded a small bottle of vodka. It was quickly shared, no more than a lick for each man, but it left us somewhat more cheerful.

A machine gun suddenly opened up on us from somewhere and we raced back to our trench, surprising a number of large rats who'd been gnawing on a body we had been too tired to bury.

One of our men had just now gotten a bullet through his thigh, but he was so numb with cold, he didn't even feel it. While I bandaged it, he pointed at my head and laughed. I reached up. I had a bullet-hole through my cap.

Night fell, and we were not sure of what to do. Stay there, or try to find our battalion? It was a serious question, not only because we might at any time have been overrun by the Japanese, but because once we had been listed officially as dead or missing, if we rejoined our unit, our category automatically would have changed to that of deserter. Which could mean the firing squad.

We decided to stay, at least for the night. Tomorrow, surely another Russian unit would arrive to occupy our positions. But we knew it wasn't safe to sleep after sunset. I don't know which we dreaded more, the Japanese or the rats. To keep warm, we built a barricade of sandbags and frozen bodies all around us and huddled together, helping one another stay awake. But sometime during the night, sleep won out. Yet we didn't freeze to death. A miracle happened. Snow fell all night and covered us so thickly, we might have dreamt we were in a feather bed at the Hotel Bristol in Petersburg.

When I awoke, the snow had nearly filled the trench. My first thought was that I had died and been buried. I suspected I was alive only from the fact that I was hungry. Slowly, I dug myself out. Even my face had been under almost a foot of snow. My comrades were still snoring. It took all my strength merely to get to my feet. Above me, there was no sky, and almost no air. It was impossible to breathe without inhaling snow, and the wind was like a knife in my lungs.

I took a little of the crisp, dry snow and washed my eyes. Now that I was upright, I could see there was not another living human being anywhere on this wide slope. My watch had stopped, and I didn't know if it was morning or afternoon. Somewhere in the distance, cannons were booming, but even the Japanese were no longer interested in our little group. I tried to use some snow to rinse out my mouth until I felt my tongue turning to ice. I envied my comrades who were still sleeping, and decided to bury myself once again in the snow. But even with a shovel I couldn't manage it. My bloodstained clothes were frozen to my body, and I couldn't loosen them without tearing off patches of skin.

Fed up with being alone in my misery, I finally tried to awaken Glasnik. But even after I had removed his thick blanket of snow, he continued to snore.

I finally awakened him by pulling his hair. He looked at me as though he'd never seen me before. It took him some time to realize where he was. Finally he helped me dig out the others. The one who had a bullet in his thigh absolutely refused to budge. I listened to his heart. It was silent as a stone.

We managed to awaken only three more soldiers, one of them Pyotr, who rather worried me, not only because he seemed full of vigor, but also because he had a slightly insane glitter in his eyes, the kind of a look you might see on a man who is ready to kill himself—or you. The others, as far as I could tell, all had died during the night. The storm was piling snow into our trench as fast as we could shovel it out. We finally decided to abandon the dead and try to find the rest of the army.

I could see some faint indications of where the road must

have been, but the snow was hip-deep and we simply didn't make any progress. If we kept going, the snow would bury us right here, and our bodies would not be found until the Chinese farmers returned for the spring planting.

We decided to go back to our trench and at least die with our comrades. But now we could no longer find the trench.

Glasnik suddenly refused to go on. Instead, he took out his *tefillin*, bared his left arm, which instantly turned as blue as skimmed milk, bound the leather straps around his arm and skull and prayed by heart, saying the *shema* in particular with all the fervor of someone bidding farewell to life. I watched him enviously. My own *tefillin* were right there in my pack, but my fingers were too frozen to unbuckle it.

Pyotr, who in Petersburg had more than once been known to tear the *tefillin* from the head of a Jewish recruit, was staring at Glasnik like a cat ready to pounce. I began to brace myself painfully for the showdown. Better this than a bullet in the back. But instead Pyotr suddenly crossed himself. Was he trying to provoke me? But as Glasnik now removed the *tefillin* and touched them to his lips, Pyotr suddenly lunged and seized them. Before I could intervene, he had kissed them, dropped to his knees, and begged them to spare his life.

While I stood open-mouthed, he handed back the *tefillin* and demanded that before he died we must forgive him for the sins he had committed against Jews. I got fed up with his whimpering and started to curse and threaten him. If I heard any more talk of dying, I said, I'd shoot him down like a dog. We had to think about saving ourselves. There's always time to die. Pyotr gave me a strange, frightened look, but calmed down.

We decided to keep moving along what appeared to be the road. The snow fell so thickly, we could barely see one another. I ordered each man to hold on to his neighbor's belt. We went on like this, part walking, part crawling.

Pyotr suddenly called my attention to a group of dark, moving figures on the horizon just ahead of us. Impossible to identify. Had the enemy cut off our last hope of escape?

We loaded our rifles and waited. The dark figures seemed to be waiting for us to make the first move. Somehow, they didn't move like Russian soldiers. I decided we could take no chances. We aimed our rifles. Half-blinded by the white steam pouring out of my mouth, I gave the order to fire. Our rifles exploded in a deafening volley. The recoil made my shoulder feel like ice struck by a hammer. I motioned the men to take cover. But there was no return fire. Nothing but a couple of high-pitched howls. Now, as they moved off, we could see they were wolves, feasting on the dead. And no doubt just waiting to make a feast of us, as well. Although they were no threat to us now, we were so incensed at their disrespect for our fallen comrades, we continued to fire until we had killed most of them.

It tore at my heart to think that, somewhere in this glacial wilderness, my brother's body might be lying exposed to the hot, sharp jaws of such creatures. But for some reason I could no longer understand why I should ever have thought of waiting to die. What greater gift was there than merely to be alive?

On we dragged through the waist-high snow. Surely, somewhere in this vast, empty country there must be some remnant of a Russian army.

All that night and the following day, afraid to abandon ourselves to the deadly seduction of sleep, we plodded through a wilderness of hills and valleys choked with unanimous snow. During the day, we were briefly encouraged to find other lost soldiers attaching themselves to our little column, numbed, half-dead, emaciated men with blackened faces, not one of whom spoke a word to anyone else.

Toward nightfall, as we gained the top of a hill, suddenly there were masses of Russian soldiers lying sprawled below us. It was a bivouac area where other refugees from the battle had begun to assemble, waiting for someone to take charge of them, to feed them, to enable them to write a few words to their families and, if it had to be, to re-form them into battleworthy units.

Drawing closer, I was startled to hear someone call my name. It was Berezin, the little Litvak from my original platoon.

We embraced one another, he demanded to know where Glasnik and I had been for the past three days, and I began asking him about our Jewish friends.

The news was mixed. Korotkin and Sinelnikoff were killed or captured in the last battle. Our strong man, Grabasz, unharmed, was now the regimental butcher. Speaking of which, my friend Rosenberg, while in the hospital, had fallen into the hands of a "tailor" who had shortened one of his legs. Krug, too, had ended up in the hospital. He had gotten a bullet through his eye and by now was probably dead.

Berezin asked me about Avrohom.

Choked, I shook my head.

Glasnik, seeing the tears in my eyes, harshly said, "For whom are you weeping? You think our end will be any better?"

I begged Berezin for some bread, which I shared with Glasnik and with Pyotr, who suddenly burst into the most bloodcurdling oaths that he would be a friend of the Jews for the rest of his days. I was frankly baffled by this passionate conversion. Glasnik's *tefillin* and my piece of bread hardly seemed enough to induce such a miraculous change of heart.

But late that night, as we sat huddled around a small fire, Pyotr, who had managed somewhere to wheedle a drink or two, came lurching over to us to insist that he owed us his life.

How did he owe us his life?

Because, in his brutish, superstitious Fonya view of the universe, it went without saying that during our long trek back from our positions, when we had countless opportunities, Glasnik and I were going to murder him. And, in his mind, it was equally obvious that only the magical powers of Glasnik's *tefillin* had somehow kept us from executing our bloody intentions.

Now, as proof that *he* no longer harbored any ill feelings toward us, he demanded Glasnik's *tefillin*, so that he might kiss them once more.

Glasnik tried to distract him; but Pyotr became more insistent, and for a moment it looked as though blood would flow after all. But, at the height of Pyotr's rage, Glasnik suddenly put a finger to his lips and, round-eyed with solemnity, explained the *tefillin* were sleeping now.

I braced myself for an eruption of drunken rage. But Pyotr merely nodded, sat down by the fire, and soon was snoring. Glasnik and I, strolling out of range, agreed it would be unwise ever to turn our backs on this man. His oaths might have sprung from a heart bursting with sincerity, but how far could one trust a man who remained convinced that only "magic" had kept us from doing to him what he would cheerfully have done to us?

17. Banzai!

It was deep winter, probably close to Hanukkah, and our regiment, after a mere two months in the bitter Manchurian wilderness, had lost more than three-fourths of its men. By now, there was no front line left to speak of. It seemed as though the Japanese were everywhere. Even our officers were more than willing to pull us back to Mukden.

But that was no longer so simple. Rearguard actions had to be fought to protect the main body, or what was left of it. Luckily for us, the enemy, acting out of some crazy Japanese notion of neatness, had paused to reorganize instead of staying on our backs and finishing the job.

Our company, which had tried without success not to end up as the rear guard, now came under steady bombardment. This enemy fire, curiously, also killed many officers. I suppose, having always been pampered, they found it hard even now to cower and grovel in muddy holes and trenches with the rest of us.

Among the replacements that belatedly started to arrive from Harbin was Vasiliev, our new company commander. He was a tall and handsome Muscovite landowner, who at once appeared to take it as a personal affront that a good percentage of his company were Jews. Were we, at a time like this, to be saddled with another Haman? He was, of course, in no position to transfer us. But we soon found out he had other ways of reducing the burden we placed on his tolerance.

One of our outposts was a desolate stretch of forest where, several times, the Japanese had crept up in the darkness and killed and mutilated our sleepy, half-starved sentries. Among our commander's first official acts was to place me in charge of this post, along with three other Jews and one new Russian boy, presumably included to keep us from talking too freely.

I was deathly tired from having been on guard duty the night before. But I could see already what kind of a bird we had here, and I wasted no breath complaining. I did, however, ask him for a machine gun to help keep us from being overrun by a surprise attack.

He gave me an aristocratic look and said, "Just go and do what you're told."

"I need a machine gun. If you'll come with us, I can show you why."

"You think I've nothing better to do? I know you Jews. You'll fall asleep and we'll lose the gun."

I tried to control my voice. "Without the gun, you may lose five men."

"Four less of you to deal with after the war," he muttered, not quite under his breath.

I felt confirmed in my suspicion that we didn't have a friend in this new Fonya, but of course what he had said was nothing more than government policy at this time. (One of the palace advisers was known to have proposed as *his* solution to the Jewish question for "one-third to emigrate, one-third to become Christians, and one-third to die." Our Vasiliev, I suspected, was interested mainly in helping ease the way for the last third.) It didn't occur to the genius that if we were killed, it would endanger the entire camp.

After supper, we proceeded to our isolated post, holding on to each others' belts in the darkness. I would not say that our spirits were exactly glowing. We knew that if we ran into trouble, we were entirely on our own. But at least our shift was only for two hours at a time.

Once we were settled in with our meager five rifles poised on rotting sandbags, my friend Glasnik, seeing my look of disgust, said, "Never mind, just wait until the next time the whole company comes under attack. One of us will see that our captain dies a hero's death."

I told him sharply in Yiddish to shut up, there was a Fonya among us. The new boy promptly answered in Yiddish, "I'm as much Fonya as you are."

Still I was distrustful. Many Russian peasants were fluent in Yiddish. I asked him to show me his *tzitzis*, the biblically-commanded fringes which, during the war, often were worn even by nonobservant Jews, if only to identify their bodies for a Jewish burial.

He opened two buttons on his tunic and told me to reach in and feel them, and we all relaxed. The new boy told us now he had known this officer for the last three months. He always sent his Jewish soldiers to the point of greatest danger, and with the same friendly explanation he gave me.

I looked at Glasnik.

"Wait till the next time we're in battle," he said with a wink. It was probably just idle talk, but I felt comforted. Although I didn't know if I could do it myself, I had no doubt that types like this officer deserved to be killed, in pure self-defense, because he was clearly prepared, night after night, to give us the most dangerous assignments until he was rid of us.

We settled down to watch and listen. Three hours later no one had come to relieve us. Somehow, I was not surprised. It was too dangerous to send back one man, and for all of us to go and desert our post might have been just what our company commander was counting on us to do. Finally, well past midnight, some shadows appeared and, being challenged, gruffly gave us the password. It was our relief. They were Russians, and they had a machine gun.

Too tired to go back to camp, we fell asleep in a nearby trench. A while later, we were awakened sharply by automatic fire. Our relief, it seemed, had all gone to sleep and one of them had been stabbed to death. But the attack consisted of only three Japanese, one of whom was killed by the machine gun; the second was wounded, and the other surrendered.

At daybreak, we all marched back together with our two captives. The wounded Japanese pitiably pleaded and gestured, but no one understood him. It seemed to me he was offering to tells us anything we wanted to know if we would let him live. One of us finally went to look for an interpreter.

Meanwhile, our commander arrived on horseback, flashing his drawn saber and grinning like a sportsman at the two Japanese, who sank to the ground and started to plead. Our commander asked for volunteers to behead the two captives. Most of the Jewish boys turned away in disgust. But the response was so enthusiastic from the others, the only solution would have been to draw lots. In the end, the commander decided he wanted to do the job himself.

A stake was driven into the ground and the captives were tied to it in a way that left their heads exposed. They were no longer pleading, but all my nerve endings could feel the hatred in their eyes.

Our commander had drawn back far enough to give his horse a running start. Now, with a shout of joy, he came galloping toward the stake. One slash and both heads plopped to the ground. Some of the men started a make-believe football game with one of the heads, while the other was picked up by a group now doing a Cossack dance and skillfully tossing it from hand to hand.

I turned away. But I realized that I, too, had already become brutalized, because I felt no more than a mild twinge of disgust.

Next morning our retreat continued, although I was no

longer at all sure we were heading in the right direction. Day and night, the sky was so thick with clouds of snow we had neither sun nor stars to guide us. Nothing but our officers' doubtful ability to read their maps and compasses.

We were still under the same orders. To stop and fight, and even counterattack, whenever conditions were favorable, and thus slow the enemy's advance toward Mukden. But with what? Our bodies? Even now our company commander still behaved as though we were heading *into* battle instead of away from it. For days no one had mentioned killing him. We were far too tired, and he was far too alert.

Glasnik turned up with the latest rumor. Alexei Kuropatkin, our minister of war, in his own person, was standing on one of the nearby hills to make a firsthand overall survey of the situation. It was said that he might take personal charge of coordinating our strategy. Strategy!

I didn't know which was worse for us, our own proud General Zasulich, who was willing to take huge losses rather than retreat in time, or Kuropatkin's policy, "No battle before we are in superior force." The second would have suited me fine, except that the Japanese refused to cooperate, and we already outnumbered them four to one.

Next day we heard that the Japanese had finished regrouping. They were ready to come after us again in full force. Since we were the closest to the enemy, we were now obliged to run the fastest. But I could see our commander was only looking for terrain in which he could halt us to fight a heroic rearguard action. Apparently, he feared he might never again get as good an opportunity to make a name for himself.

Their artillery had now found our range, which meant their forward observers must have been quite close to us. And yet we could never spot one.

Darkness fell, but their accurate shelling never let up. We were obliged to keep running. Toward dawn, a messenger from headquarters came riding up. We had suddenly been ordered to stop and make a stand.

Our company commander was justly furious. Here the terrain was flat and almost indefensible. We'd passed up far better positions to which it was now too late to return. But headquarters was adamant. The enemy was advancing too quickly. Time had to be gained to reinforce Mukden.

The ground was icy and rocky. It was impossible for us to dig trenches. Our commander ordered us instead to build ramparts out of frozen corpses, the only material with which we were generously supplied.

During the night, while small Japanese units leapfrogged toward us in quick, terrifying little spurts, the wall in front of me unexpectedly collapsed. It seemed one of the frozen bodies we had used was not yet dead and had moved his legs. Before we could think of repairing the breach, our commander ordered us to counterattack.

Much as I disliked him, I had to admit the man thought like a soldier. That is, in theory his instincts were correct. If we were fresh troops, properly equipped, he might well have brought it off, caught the enemy out in the open, and perhaps even given them a bloody nose. But most of us were totally spent, and wanted no part of his mad scheme, even if we had had normal artillery support, reserves, and enough ammunition.

Now a sensible officer, knowing all this, would have pulled in his horns. It must have been dead plain that we were in no shape to be inspired or threatened.

But our commander was not a man to take no for an answer. He worked himself into an almost insane fury, and suddenly he was firing his revolver point-blank at those who had made no move to get into position.

Several men were hit, and the others jumped to obey. Glasnik whispered, "We should have shot him during the last bombardment."

I, just as angry, vowed, "He'll never see Russia again."

By the time we were finally set to counterattack, it was daybreak. The Japanese were firmly entrenched behind our own abandoned barbed wire, and when the sun came up it would be directly in our eyes.

The whole enterprise was now, of course, sheer lunacy, and I assumed even our commander would have sense enough to call it off.

He didn't dream of it. What's more, he ordered me now to take five men with wirecutters and open a breach in the barbed wire. He had reloaded his revolver, and it was either that or get shot.

Nevertheless, I told him, "It's too light already. We'll never reach the barbed wire."

He waved the revolver in my face and shouted, "Go on, Jew. Go on. Before I make an example of you, too."

I looked at the other soldiers. Like sheep, they were ready to go, more afraid of his revolver than of the Japanese machine guns. I blindly picked five men, and led the way without even bothering to see if they were following.

My prediction turned out to have been too pessimistic. By inching forward on my stomach, I did reach the barbed wire. But I knew that the moment I rose up and started to cut it, I'd be an easy target. Still, now that I was here, what should I do?

I looked back uncertainly at our lines, and could see our commander surveying the enemy positions. None of my five "volunteers" had bothered to keep up with me, and if I took a shot at Vasiliev now, no one could say it was not an enemy bullet.

I slowly crawled around until I could aim my rifle. The barbed wire could wait. My only fear was that he'd climb back down from his vantage point. I had him in my sights now, but for some reason couldn't press the trigger. My hand was either cramped or frozen stiff. I was rubbing it against my tunic to restore circulation, when I heard the scream of the first shell. As I lay pressed against the icy mud, still facing to the rear, I could tell by the flashes that we were being pounded by our own artillery.

It was only after several minutes that they seemed to realize their range was too short. I found out later that it was our commander, the man I had been about to kill, who managed to signal our artillery to cease firing.

Meanwhile, at least there was no further talk about the counterattack, because, with the first beams of sunlight, hordes of Japanese had risen out of the earth and, like a tidal wave, come rolling steadily toward us, accompanied by queer blasts on a bugle and a roar of voices raised in a single word, *"Banzai!"*

Our company disintegrated before my eyes. We turned and ran, stumbling heedlessly over dead and wounded alike. Far behind us, from time to time, we heard a hideous shriek, which I assumed to be one of our wounded being done to death.

I hadn't yet forgotten our commander who, after a furious, pistol-waving attempt to rally us, now was running as fast as any man in the company. I had trouble catching up to him until suddenly he staggered. A bullet had torn his neck. He tried to keep running, which was a mistake, because he ran right into an explosion which tore off part of his leg.

I was suddenly the closest to him and instinctively I picked him up and slung him over my back. At once, I heard two men behind me shout, "The dog! Let him rot!"

As I stumbled forward, trying not to fall, he gasped, "God bless the Jews! Dear God, let me live, so that I may earn their forgiveness."

He babbled on like this, while my comrades, Jew and gentile, muttered behind my back. "Throw him down, the filthy dog!" they said. "Hasn't he killed enough of us?"

They were absolutely right, of course. Yet somehow, having done this much, I felt I couldn't just drop him now. To a Jew, after all, a *baal-teshuvah*, a repentant one, is said to rank higher even than a man of lifelong piety. I didn't know how literally one should take this, or even whether this only applied to Jews, and I was nagged by the suspicion that my commander's repentance might not have been altogether sincere. But who was I to judge another human soul?

With each step, my company commander's weight seemed to double, like some demon out of an old wives' tale trying to test a weak man's resolve. Although it must have been agony for him to talk, he plainly felt his life depended on keeping me reassured of how much he now loved the Jews.

We stumbled on past wounded men pleading with us either to take them along or to kill them. Large rats could be seen gnawing at the dead and almost dead, whose bodies were contorted like jugglers, or like sneak thieves frozen in mid-motion and powdered by erratic drifts of snow. But none of us was able to think of anything beyond staying on his feet.

I suddenly felt a bullet barely miss my head. When I turned, I saw the company commander was dead.

I didn't want to notice whose gun was smoking. Russian or Jew, whoever did it, I merely hoped he wasn't trying to kill me as well. Feeling disgusted with my men, but also relieved, I bent over sideways and let the commander's body slide to the ground. His warm, sticky blood had soaked through my tunic. I tried to wipe it off the back of my neck before it froze.

For the rest of that day, I could not get myself to look anyone in the face. Not even Glasnik, who I was sure was innocent. Because with all my loose talk about killing him, not to mention my own halfhearted attempt, I felt now like an accomplice to the murder.

18. This Way to the Firing Squad

Our retreat on Mukden finally had lost some of its nightmarish quality of headlong flight. Mainly because, after weeks on the run, with virtually no food or sleep, we were worn down to the point where we'd not only ceased to resemble an army, but barely still invited comparison with human beings.

Meanwhile, Kuropatkin had now taken personal charge of stemming the tide in the Harbin-Mukden sector. Usually, in our army when a new man took over, he felt obliged at once to produce some victories, regardless of cost. In fact, Kuropatkin's first order of the day was, "We will spare neither blood nor treasure; all must be sacrificed for Emperor and Fatherland." But he took just one look at the leftovers of our battalion, and had us taken out of the line and quartered in an abandoned village.

This didn't mean we were left free to recuperate. Although we moved about like shadows, there were still enough officers around to see that outward appearances were maintained. One of these was guard duty.

A call went out for all noncoms to report to the commandant.

I made believe I hadn't heard. For me, the final straw had been the week before when, under attack and almost out of ammunition, I'd been ordered to take a white flag and surrender the company to what, in the end, turned out to be a Russian unit. But this recognition had not come until we had shelled each other enthusiastically for some hours and they, in their final blind charge, had been only inches from bayoneting me, white flag and all.

For my conduct in this lunatic affair, or maybe just to keep my mouth shut about it, the new commander himself had assured me of a medal. But I'd decided I was finished with responsibility. Let them take my stripe. The pay, which we rarely received and had no place to spend, could never make up for all the aggravation, danger, and lost sleep. I was ready to lie down and not get up for a month. But before I had a chance to get myself demoted, one of the lieutenants tracked me down. I was told to take ten soldiers and mount guard. I told him I hadn't slept all week, to let me rest at least one night.

He was not unsympathetic, but explained there was a shortage of noncoms. I must do my duty and help fill the gap.

It was a beautiful clear night with no more than a mild breeze. Having deployed my ten men, and sternly warned them not to close an eye, I was tempted for a moment to sit down. But that, of course, was strictly forbidden, and I knew I would not remember to get up again. Nevertheless, my lids kept drooping. To hold them open, I pinched myself, I kicked one foot against the other, and generally struggled like a man about to drown.

Near midnight, I was awakened roughly by a strange officer and two armed men. The officer demanded to know where my gun was. My heart stopped. I was without a rifle. There was no sign of it anywhere. We were miles from any Japanese. One of our own men must have stolen it.

Fifteen minutes later, the new commander who, only two days earlier, had lauded my coolness under fire, told me what I didn't need to be told. The penalty for sleeping on guard was the same as that for losing one's rifle: death. About my only comfort was they couldn't kill me twice.

The captain lectured me on what he thought of such undisciplined, irresponsible soldiers as myself. But he allowed that, of course, from a Jew, what else could you expect? I noticed I was not a Jew two days ago, when he was promising to recommend me for a medal.

I was put into an improvised jail cell under heavy guard. The survivors of my company, however, were furious. From behind my bars, I could hear snatches of their reassuring arguments, not only about the injustice being done to me, but also their sporting curiosity about whether I'd be shot or get away with twenty-five years at hard labor.

Despite such stimulating thoughts, I slept like a corpse until noon the following day. It was only now that I was somewhat rested that I began to see the full depth of the trouble I was in. Three days ago I hadn't much cared if I lived or died. But now, having regained some of my strength, I also had gotten back all my old appetite to go on living.

Had I served Mother Russia all these years, only now to be shot to death by my own comrades? Especially hard to bear since less than a month ago my closest brother Avrohom was lost in action. Were my parents to lose *two* of their sons in this folly of a war?

When they brought my ration of bread and water for lunch, I left it untouched. My heart was so bitter, I felt I would choke on a drop of water.

In the evening, Glasnik stopped at my window and consoled me with the news that I was the principal topic of conversation all over the camp. While most of the Russian boys were fairly nonchalant about my fate, the Jewish soldiers insisted, as a matter of principle, that I must not be executed. They'd circulated petitions asking men to sign a statement that they would refuse to shoot me. Those who wouldn't sign their names were warned that whoever took part in my firing squad would not live to return to Russia.

Since we Jews were somewhat in the minority, I not only felt proud of them, but also concerned that some of my friends might yet end up standing next to me against the wall.

But strangely enough, the officers began to get a little nervous. Accustomed for years to shooting deserters and other delinquents without hearing a word of complaint, they realized that mine was not going to be a routine case.

Their uneasiness, of course, was not the result of my popularity, or of fear of their Jewish soldiers. It was that their confidence in themselves as a class had been shaken by the recent succession of military disasters. They also couldn't help but be mindful of the current revolutionary ferment back home. (This had already led to hundreds of government-inspired pogroms, but at long last, had also shown Jews capable of organized and effective self-defense.) Anyway, the order was passed down that none of my guards were to be Jews.

Unfortunately, my old defender, Prince Mikhailoff, was believed to be in Harbin, and there was one adjutant of whom, back in Petersburg, while both of were somewhat drunk, I had been clumsy enough to make an enemy. (It was a little incident for which he couldn't have me court-martialed then, because he would have had to explain what he was doing with another officer's wife.)

Now it turned out that he had neither forgotten nor forgiven me for my unintentional rudeness. And, with an efficiency which, if applied to his own duties, would quickly have made him at least a general, he rushed through the paper work required to send me into the next world.

Glasnik, beside himself, raised his right hand and swore by Heaven and earth that if the adjutant signed the order for my execution, he, Glasnik, would kill him personally and then put a bullet through his own head.

I begged him not to do anything that not only could no longer do *me* any good, but might cause difficulties for other Jewish soldiers.

Meanwhile, five guards approached, leading a chained prisoner who was to share my hut. He was tall, taciturn, and eagle-nosed, but with some strange, livid marks on the tip of his nose.

"Where are you from, brother?" I asked him.

"Gruziya."

"And what is it they want from you?"

He spit and shrugged. "Let them shoot me. I've done what I had to do."

He was a mountain dweller, and his people were not noted for their patience. What had he done? It seems that one of his officers, when drunk, would amuse himself by stubbing out his lighted cigarette on this soldier's nose, the size of which appeared to offend him.

Well, one day, after the officer had repeated this game two or three times, my fellow prisoner lunged for the man's sword and lopped off his head.

I congratulated him, but suspected his chances of getting shot were even better than mine.

Like me, he had little appetite for his bread and water. But he slept soundly enough, while I didn't manage to doze off until long past midnight.

When I awoke, I found him wrapped in a *tallis*, saying his morning prayers. I jumped up, rinsed my hands, got my own *tallis* and *tefillin*, and tried to keep up with him. But his melodies and his style of pronunciation were so exotic to me, in the end I simply stood and listened to him until he was finished.

Now, for the first time, we shook hands. I addressed him in Yiddish. He looked at me blankly and replied in Hebrew. So we ended up once more speaking Russian to each other.

I spent the day "doctoring" him, that is, carefully enlarging the scorch marks on his nose until his whole face looked swollen and grotesque. That way, when he went on trial, perhaps the judge would recognize that, after such hideous abuse, even the mildest of men might reach for a sword. The Georgian doubted it would do the slightest bit of good. But he saw I was dying of boredom and anxiety, and so he good-naturedly allowed me to distract myself with his nose.

The next day, early in the morning, both of us were taken in chains to a nearby town, where a military court was sitting to judge us. Both of us were given defense attorneys. My friend's lawyer seemed quite capable, and I was proud to see he made the most of his client's now really dreadful-looking nose.

About my own attorney, I was less enthusiastic. The one thing he wouldn't even consider was that I simply tell the truth —that a human being can go only so long without sleep. Of course, he probably knew his customers and what they would believe and what they wouldn't. He seemed to feel my only possible defense was to claim that, owing to food poisoning or drinking polluted water, I now suffered from a strange sickness which, without warning, could send me into a coma.

Frankly, I was desperate enough to try anything. But where on this green earth would I find a Russian army doctor who would favor me with such an improbable diagnosis?

My counsel agreed it wouldn't be easy. Especially since none of the doctors at this post were known to be Jews. But he was still making inquiries. So that was what my life depended on: a nonexistent Jewish doctor.

The court, after hearing my attorney's preposterous story, surprised me. They agreed to postpone my case until I'd had a thorough medical examination. I felt even more hopeful when I saw that the Georgian got off with only five years at hard labor. He was ecstatic and threw me a kiss as they led him out.

I had one more night in my cell, guarded like the crown jewels. Tomorrow an army doctor would determine whether I really suffered from such a mysterious illness. Even my attorney admitted, if the doctor found me healthy, it was the firing squad.

Alone once more, I was seized by depression. I cursed my

attorney for not having let me tell the truth. There were plenty of fresh troops to mount guard. Why pick on a man who'd barely slept a minute during the week-long retreat?

Late in the evening, a middle-aged lieutenant suddenly arrived to take me away. I was surprised to recognize him as a man for whom my brother Mordechai, back in Petersburg, had bought many a glass of vodka. Could he be here now to return the favor? If not, would it be tactful to remind him who I was? But his manner was so cold and forbidding, I kept silent.

He marched me with chained hands in the direction of the officers' quarters. Halfway there, he slowed his pace, moved up beside me and, without any change of expression, told me not to be frightened. "I'm only taking you to the doctor."

"This time of night?"

"One of *your* doctors," he said in a whisper. "He's expecting you."

I still didn't trust him. My attorney might dream of miracles, but Glasnik had checked once more that afternoon and assured me there were no Jewish doctors at this post, or anywhere nearby.

The lieutenant explained to me that this one was a converted Jew, which to him was plainly one and the same thing.

I, on the other hand, knew that men who have turned themselves from bad Jews into bad Christians are in fact apt to bend over backwards to show they are untainted by old loyalties. But go explain that to a Russian officer. In any event, I had little choice in the matter.

Presently, I saw I was not being taken to the hospital but directly to the doctor's house. I considered that a mistake. It was late at night and the doctor would either be angry at being disturbed, or the whole thing would look so conspiratorial, he'd feel himself compromised.

At the doctor's house, there was some kind of party going on inside. Through the window we could see our doctor with half a dozen fellow officers. They were eating, drinking, playing cards. It was quite obvious he was not expecting anyone like me.

My escort cursed under his breath. There was nothing to do but take me back to my cell. He said, somewhat grudgingly, he'd come for me again when the party was over. But his manner now, as he marched back, was so furtive and jumpy, I realized he had done all this at some risk to himself. Clearly, it would be even more conspicuous if he came back for me later at night.

I lay down on my bunk and tormented myself, wondering if the convert-doctor had been playing a cruel joke on me, or whether he had given in momentarily to a charitable impulse, and then either changed his mind or simply forgotten all about it.

Somewhat to my surprise, an hour past midnight my door was unlocked, and the same lieutenant, even more sternly than before, told me to come with him.

We slunk through the camp like a pair of thieves. My heart was pounding as we approached the doctor's quarters. All the lights were out. He was probably asleep by now and would be furious at being awakened. But by this time, I didn't care any longer.

I hid in the shadows while the officer rapped on the door. The doctor finally appeared in his nightshirt. As I expected, he was in a rage at having been awakened. His irritation was even greater when he found out it was not an emergency at the hospital, but merely a matter of life and death for a Jewish soldier. Still hidden, I prayed silently for the merits of my holy and beloved ancestors to intercede for me.

The convert finally deigned to let me into his house. He looked me up and down and pronounced, "There isn't a thing in the world wrong with this man." He was clearly ready to usher us right back out.

I stood my ground and replied, rather insolently, "Maybe there is, and maybe there isn't."

Now a man with any spark of Jewish feeling would at once have responded to an observation like that. But the doctor only got more annoyed. "What are *your* medical qualifications?"

"Who knows how I feel better than I?"

"And that gives you the right to come and wake me in the middle of the night?" If he talked any louder, he would rouse every officer on the street.

"I thought you understood," I said, more subdued. "I'm under sentence of death."

"What's that to me?"

I turned helplessly to my escort. He shrugged. He'd done his share. He was ready to take me back.

But now it seemed that the doctor knew all along what I was there for. Perhaps he wanted to demonstrate that he was now a good Orthodox Russian, and no longer a member of what our sages have called *rakhmonim bnei rakhmonim*, "the merciful children of the merciful."

"Why did you fall asleep on guard?" he demanded.

I started to tell him how I hadn't slept for several nights, but I caught a warning look from my escorting officer just in time. So I quickly launched into a recital of how I'd eaten some spoiled meat and drunk polluted water, and that night, while on guard, had had convulsions and had suddenly lost consciousness.

The doctor looked at me with what I couldn't help but regard as Jewish skepticism. "You look healthy enough to me now."

"Thank God, I'm feeling a little better," I hastened to assure him.

"Perhaps imprisonment agrees with you."

My hopes evaporated. He was only playing with me. Of course. How could a creature like a convert leave himself open to the suspicion of helping a Jew? I bit my lip and stared at him with open contempt. I had no intention of begging a swine like that for my life.

He folded his hands behind him, marched up and down in front of me like an actor on a stage, and studied me with an expression of great shrewdness. I could feel my life hanging on his mood, his whim, perhaps his own fears. After a long silence, he said, "Get back to your unit."

I didn't quite understand what this meant, but outside, my

lieutenant hugged me with relief. As we returned to my platoon area, I found some of my friends were up and waiting for me.

But the officer of the guard, in the absence of written orders, refused to release me. I still had to spend the night in my cell. However, I was allowed to take with me a cup of water filled with vodka furnished by my friends.

At daybreak, I was awakened. Two men with bared swords were standing over me.

My heart almost jolted to a stop. They told me to put on my boots; they'd come to escort me back to the tribunal.

I stood once more before my judges, and couldn't keep my eyes off the adjutant who had worked so diligently to have me shot. He smirked like a man who knew more than I did.

I had told my attorney what the convert-doctor had said, and he now repeated his defense about my strange illness and offered to support this with expert testimony.

The adjutant laughed in his face. I couldn't understand why, until I saw how well he had prepared himself. No less than four army doctors were ready to examine me on the spot. I looked frantically around for my convert. Although he had hardly received me like a brother, I'd begun to feel, as they say, "It's better to deal with a familiar thief than with a strange rabbi." Sympathetic or not, at least this convert understood the situation. But now there was not a hair of him to be seen. May *your* life never hang on the whim of a turncoat.

In less time than it took for me to undo my top button, the four doctors pronounced me in perfect health. No need even to open my tunic for them. Bewildered, I was beginning to wonder if I dreamt the events of last night.

But my attorney now proved not to be a complete fool at all. He had run quickly over to the clinic, burst in on my doctor, and dragged him away from a roomful of patients. When they returned, I was relieved to see that my convert outranked the other four doctors.

He, too, examined me right then and there. What he did was

roughly separate my lids and shine a match in front of my eyes. His fingers reeked of tobacco. I felt my lashes being singed. His eyes stabbed into mine like a surgeon's knife. The devil only knows what he expected to find there. Behind me, the adjutant snickered. I flinched as the convert suddenly turned to his colleagues and shouted, "How can you say this man is well. Have you examined his brain?"

Flustered, the other doctors shook their heads. I could see they were skeptical but, thank Heaven, in Fonya's army, you didn't argue with a superior officer.

"You never noticed there is a spot on his brain?"

"And what is the significance of that?" demanded the presiding judge, who outranked even my doctor friend.

"That spot is a symptom of a kind of sleeping sickness." He said it so convincingly that for a moment I wondered how long I could live with such a disease. "A man with those symptoms may sink into a coma at any moment. He should never have been allowed to serve in the army. But now that he's here, the only place for him is the hospital."

He told the other doctors to look into my eyes, and each of them dutifully lighted a match, agreed with his diagnosis, and apologized to the court for having overlooked my brain. I was furnished hastily with a chair, and began to enjoy all this sudden solicitude.

My convert, before returning to the clinic, warned the court that such a spot on the brain, if not properly treated, could lead not only to sleeping sickness but to insanity.

The presiding officer, with a disgusted look, ordered me straight to the hospital for observation and treatment. I was not convinced that he believed a word of all this, but form had been satisfied, and probably if I could produce such influential supporters, it was best not to shoot me.

I assumed that now that the court-martial had found me not guilty, all of the hospital nonsense would be quietly forgotten, and I'd go back to my unit. But my doctor seemed to have enjoyed his little joke too much to let it end there. Clearly, the Jewish spark in him was still far from dead.

I was sent to a hospital in Mukden, where I met a number of my old comrades, some of them badly maimed, but all delighted to be out of the war. They told me how some units, owing to inadequate supplies or tactical blunders, were slaughtered even worse than ours. So a soldier who lost only an arm or a foot felt that the rest of his body was pure profit.

I was assigned a bed, examined by a brain specialist, and given food such as milk and white bread whose taste I had long forgotten. In fact, I was given everything but medicine.

After a while, it dawned on me that the doctors here knew it was all a put-up job, but weren't sure who was behind it. So, to avoid trouble, they kept me among the critically ill and the dying, and I ended up eating not only my own food, but theirs as well.

Eight days of this golden life, and I was abruptly pronounced cured and sent back to my company.

I reported to the officer who had started all my troubles by putting me on guard duty. He wanted me to assure him that I was totally cured and in no danger of relapse.

I told him, "How can I be sure? All I know is the doctors in Mukden said that I'm fit for duty again."

My officer shook his head worriedly. Someone must have given him hell for entrusting the safety of the camp to a man with spots on the brain. He said, "Well, just make sure you get enough sleep. And don't, for heaven's sake, fall out of bed."

19. The Second Road to the Left

Back from the hospital, I found the remnants of our tattered battalion overrun by hundreds upon hundreds of starved and demoralized survivors from General Kuropatkin's latest "counteroffensive." (This was yet another one of those impulsive gambles undertaken on the basis of only the most haphazard sort of intelligence—furnished solely by our colorful and brave but hopelessly undisciplined Cossack cavalry.) The growing number of these unexpected guests had of course quickly wiped out what was left of our meager provisions.

What did our officers do? Instead of encouraging or even forcing the newcomers to go elsewhere, some colonel (with a typical Fonya sense of propriety) got up on a table and announced that anyone caught leaving the area would be shot.

To make quite sure we didn't overlook anyone worth shooting, we noncoms were put to work writing down everyone's name and other statistics.

All went smoothly until I came upon a bear of a Cossack with long, vicious spurs on his boots, who stood near a tree with his eyes half-closed and not only didn't answer my questions, but ignored me altogether.

"Name and unit?" I shouted at him once more, getting annoyed.

Not a word out of him.

So to preserve my authority, I unloaded on him the kind of *mi-sheberach* a Russian noncom kept handy for those who didn't jump at his command. In the middle of this, he carefully took three steps backwards, turns to me and, in the purest Lithuanian Yiddish, mildly demanded, "What are you getting so angry about? Didn't you see I couldn't talk?"

By and by, over a chew of tobacco, my Cossack admitted that he was ordinarily a bit more handy with horses and guns than with afternoon prayers. In fact, as a young man, when no one was listening, he even used to say out loud sometimes, "There is no God," and would find this theory confirmed by not being instantly struck dead. (As you see, when a Litvak goes astray, he goes, as they say in America, whole hog.)

As it happened, shortly before, as part of our great "counter-offensive," his squadron had been ordered to make a lancer charge at midnight against a Japanese encampment. The only problem was no one had told his officers where to find the Japanese. So he had volunteered to go out alone and scout for them. Not, he hastened to explain, out of patriotism or bravery, but because he'd recently been awarded a beautiful medal for something or other, and he liked it so much he wanted another one.

After blundering around on horseback for most of the night, he hadn't found the Japanese, but at sunrise they had found him. And had begun to lay down such a barrage as could very nicely have taken care of his whole regiment.

Pinned down, with no hope of escape, he had seriously considered killing himself. (And perhaps I should explain here that our frequent readiness to consider suicide was, unlike today, not a sign of madness or despair, but simply the weighing of a reasonable alternative over something worse.) However, with good Litvak logic, he figured he might as well try to make a run for it. After all, how could he lose? If there was no God, he'd be killed anyway; and if there was, here was His chance to prove it!

But to make it a fair test, he vowed, like a man gambling buttons against diamonds, that if, by some miracle, he should come through unharmed, he would without fail pray three times daily for the rest of his life.

And here, while he was trying to keep his vow at least for the first few days, *I* had to come and shout at him like a wild man.

Why am I telling you all this? It turned out that the units held in reserve for this particular counterattack also included the survivors of the Third Company, First Novocherkassky Regiment, to which my brother Avrohom had belonged. But that was all he could tell me. He had no idea where I could find them now.

It had been a good many months since I reconciled myself to the likelihood that Avrohom was dead. Yet, hearing that some fraction of his company had survived, I was suddenly flooded with fresh hope and determined to locate this remnant.

But before I could arrange for a pass, we unexpectedly received several cartloads of food, blankets, and ammunition, and when I woke up in the morning there was a row of kettles boiling a soup which deserved to be called soup only because what we saw floating on its surface were not tea leaves.

For the moment, of course, most of us barely remembered what it felt like to have something warm in our bellies. With our bowls and big wooden spoons, we started at once to form long, impatient lines. Only there was one little problem. Last week our officers had requisitioned food for us and for the eighteen hundred or so stragglers we had on our books. Since then, however, that number had almost tripled. Now when it was announced that soup could be served only to those whose names had previously been registered, there was a riot, and we found ourselves suddenly divided into two armies.

The men who were entitled to eat set up machine guns to

guard the kettles, while the newcomers withdrew with their rifles, took cover, and let us know that unless everyone received an equal share, they'd shoot the kettles full of holes and no one would get anything.

The water started to boil, along with our tempers, and of course our officers were nowhere in sight.

Under the circumstances, I myself would have thought it wisest to give everyone, entitled or not, an equal share. But I couldn't deny Glasnik's logic that if these few kettles of soup were to be divided fairly among more than five thousand men, it would come out roughly to one spoonful of soup for every ten men.

Fortunately, the Russian soldier is not famous for his initiative, and for the moment everyone still waited for our officers to make a move. Not that, Heaven forbid, we expected them to come up with some Solomonic solution to the conflict. We simply wanted to see them dare to take their traditional places at the head of the line.

For once, though, even they were smart enough to realize that the first officer to fill his bowl with soup would end up with so many holes in him, the soup would never reach his stomach.

But leave it to the Russian officer mentality.

A nearby artillery unit was induced to drop a couple of shells at the very edge of our camp. While everyone scurried for cover, a number of trusted men hastily hauled the kettles to a more easily defensible location, set up their machine guns, and actually succeeded in feeding at least a portion of those men who were entitled to stand in line. That is, they got to share whatever was left after our officers had had their turn.

And this was how *Batyushka Tsar* fed his defenders under battlefield conditions.

Many of us now realized that, if we didn't want to starve, we'd have to go into business for ourselves, either by exercising the traditional Russian talent for foraging (that is, robbing helpless Chinese farmers at gunpoint), or by drifting away to search for another camp where a hot meal might not be quite such an exciting novelty.

However, since my Jewish Cossack friend believed that my brother's company might still be somewhere in this sector, I decided to stay where I was.

Meanwhile, my company, which was now down to maybe a fifth of its original strength, had been waiting anxiously for the railroad to have pity and bring us fresh soldiers to replace the ones our generals had used up. And at last, we did get our first carload of reservists. They turned out for the most part to be elderly homebodies burdened with anxiety for their wives and children, and they fit in with us veterans about as smoothly as a hunchback fits against a wall.

The revolutionaries among them also had some very pretty stories to tell about new riots, massacres, strikes, mutinies, and pogroms back in the mother country. None of this added to my enthusiasm for my present job, which was to take these sad creatures they had sent us and drill them into ferocious soldiers ready to die rather than let General Oyama march into Mukden.

I was, at this time, altogether going through a period of depression, harrowed by dreams which were so real, I was certain they were trying to tell me something. But what? Having lost Avrohom, the one brother to whom I'd always felt closest, and without one letter from home in more than eight months, I'd begun to suspect, with daily growing certainty, that the outbreak of so many officially inspired pogroms which followed "Bloody Sunday" in Petersburg must also have claimed the lives of my parents. After all, if they were still alive, would not at least one of them have written me in all this time?

These gloomy thoughts led in turn to morbid fantasies in which I saw myself surviving the war, but as a helpless invalid, and coming home to find not a single relative left alive who might look after me. And I wondered, would I too turn into one of those wretched, fiery-eyed, crippled beggars I remembered from my youth in Warsaw, men maimed in the Russo-Turkish War, groveling in the streets like savage stray dogs?

While in this bitter frame of mind, I forgot, of course, that no one else in my company had received mail in eight months either.

One morning, despite our army's slipshod ways with forwarding anything less exciting than ammunition, we found several sacks of mail had arrived for our company.

Just as my father had once done in our home town because our regular mailman couldn't read, I was now appointed to call out the names on the letters. Before long, our happiness was tainted by other emotions. Almost eight out of ten recipients were no longer there to respond to their names, and no one knew the forwarding address to the Other World.

I read names for half an hour, and not one of the letters was for me. My old nightmare fears began to choke me once again. I found myself trembling, hardly able to read aloud. Among the last handful of letters I twice shouted out the name "Marateck" before I realized it was for me.

Some of the men, unable to read, had been kissing the letters or pressing them to their hearts. Now that mail call was over, they begged me to read their letters to them. But right now I had no head for anything but the envelope addressed in my father's hand.

I sat down somewhere and read:

My dear son Jacob,

This letter is not written with ink but with tears. So many months have gone by, this is already my twelfth letter and not a word from either you or Avrohom. Some people say that your entire regiment has been wiped out, but we can only think what has become of our two sons. Every minute is to us like a year. Your mother and your aunts run every day to pray upon the graves of their holy parents to intercede for you Up There. We spend whole days only awaiting the mailman. I try to console your mother that God will help and He will bring a good message. But deep in my heart I am afraid, because I know it cannot be that both of you have forgotten your parents. I no longer know what it is to sleep nights, but I still say *tehillim* for you daily, and so do the Rebbe and all his Hasidim, that you may be preserved from the great danger you are in. Dear son, if, Heaven forbid, anything has happened to either one of you, I beg you to write us the truth, that we may know the worst. We greet you, your father and mother who hope to hear good news, Amen.

Shloime Zalman Marateck

I sat down with paper and pencil and, without waiting for my tears to dry, at once replied that we both were, praised be His Name, in good health, only Avrohom was unable to enclose a greeting at the moment because he'd just gone to town to buy tobacco.

Having written this and handed it to the mail clerk, I was gripped by a ferocious determination somehow to turn my lie into truth. In what we all now knew to be little better than a complete rout, tens of thousands of missing Russian soldiers must surely have been scattered all over Manchuria, in hospitals, villages, Japanese prison camps, or temporarily attached to other units. If Avrohom was still alive somewhere, I was resolved to find him, even if, during my search for him, I was listed as a deserter.

Happily, my old defender, Prince Mikhailoff, had just returned from Harbin to become acting regimental commander.

I don't know what, if anything, he'd heard about my latest court-martial, but as soon as he saw me he dragged me into his office, filled me up with vodka, and presented me with half a loaf of bread.

Frankly, I didn't understand why, after all this time, he should still take an interest in me. Unless, as had been previously suspected, he did have some Jewish blood in him. In fact, after several drinks, I felt light-headed enough to ask him this insolent question.

To my surprise, all he said was, "I honestly don't know. I suppose it's possible. All I know is at times I feel more drawn to your people than I do to my own class. But I beg you to keep this to yourself."

And to this day, I have kept his secret, although shortly thereafter he, too, was killed in action.

I told him now why I had come to see him. It was six months since I had heard from my brother Avrohom and, for my parents' sake and my own, I *had* to know whether he was dead or alive.

Mikhailoff explained to me that the transport containing all the records of the Third Company, First Novocherkassky Regiment had been captured by the Japanese. So I would simply have to wait for news about my brother until the war was over.

I refused to accept this. I stressed I was not asking out of mere curiosity. But I had sworn to my parents I would look out for my younger brother, even as, in Scripture, Judah had vowed to his father that, if he returned from Egypt without Benjamin, his own life would be forfeit *forever* (which Rashi explains to mean "even in the World-to-Come"). Now, if Avrohom was dead, how could I ever face my parents again?

Mikhailoff, Heaven knew why, seemed strangely moved by my Jewish illogic, and especially by my citation of Judah's later words to Joseph, "For how shall I return to my father and the lad is not with me, and how shall I look upon his grief?" He instantly dispatched no less than three riders to the nearest telegraph station, with messages ordering all commanders to check whether, among their wounded or stragglers from other units, the name Avrohom Marateck was listed.

Along with the mail, we'd received some three-month-old Petersburg newspapers, which were kind enough to inform us that our army was almost on the verge of expelling every last Japanese soldier from the Asiatic mainland. (In fact, one got the impression that only the Czar's infinite kindness kept us from driving out all the Chinese as well.)

The only uncensored news we had from home was a little magazine in Yiddish which printed a kind of comic strip about the adventures of a scrawny little man called "Uncle Pinye" or "Pintshik" and his gigantic wife "Raizel," and it took no great cleverness to figure out that "Pintshik" was Japan *(der Yapantshik)* and "Meema Raizel" was *Matushka Rossiya* (Mother Russia). Under the guise of their little domestic tiffs, in which Raizel mercilessly bullied Pinye, but her little husband always got the best of her, it was conveyed to us that not everyone back home was taken in by the disgusting lies and boasts of the censored press.

During this time of idleness, while we waited impatiently for the American president (Theodore Roosevelt) to help negotiate an end to this war, and several soldiers continued to be killed each day by Japanese snipers or Chinese bandits, we were still being exhorted to prepare ourselves, physically and spiritually, for the decisive battle of Mukden. This, we were told, would determine the outcome of the war once and for all, and teach the upstart Japanese a lesson they would not forget for centuries to come. Which was that, as General Kuropatkin had lately inscribed on his banner, "The Lord Preserves His Own."

To raise our morale, we were also informed in strict secrecy that, unknown to our treacherous enemy, a vast Russian fleet under Admiral Makaroff had been sent all the way around Africa to come upon the Japanese from behind and blow them out of the water. (What actually happened, as I read many years later, was that, in May, after months of hardship, incompetence, and all sorts of bad luck, when the Russian fleet—actually under Admiral Rozhdestvenski—finally appeared in the Strait of Tsushima, the Japanese navy lost no time at all in sending it straight to the bottom.)

But while I went on training our pitiful replacements and we all waited with great enthusiasm for the "Battle of Destiny," no unit anywhere, despite all Colonel Mikhailoff's efforts, seemed to have any record of an Avrohom Marateck. Of course, I knew it was time I faced reality, but I refused to reconcile myself to his death and, in my gloom and bitterness, I made life hell for our unfortunate reservists.

One afternoon someone came running with the news that

he'd discovered a ruined Cathayan village that some enterprising Chinese had put back in operation. Specifically, what they'd done was open up a number of establishments in which one could get a drink. And while, admittedly, their schnapps, by our standards, might have had a rather foul breath, we were assured it was guaranteed to make you drunk, which was all the assurance most of us needed. What was more, the village also had attractions of another sort.

Full of reproach at the Almighty, who taught us how to be holy and how to govern our "inclinations," but not how to keep others from trampling on our lives, as well as fatigued from yet another day of mutual torture, in which I had tried, sadistically, again and again, to teach our apathetic recruits how to make a bayonet charge against a trench defended by machine guns, I promptly volunteered to let myself be guided to this oasis of wickedness.

The promised "kilometer or two" to the village took us only about two hours, since at night we had to move with some caution to avoid being ambushed, not only by the enemy but also by some of our Chinese "allies."

Otherwise everything was as advertised, and one could indeed get drunk there at a reasonable cost, especially once the alcohol had sufficiently paralyzed your sense of smell. Among those who accosted us on the street was an elderly Chinese. He had a kind of magic lantern in which, for five kopeks, one could see things not usually seen in army camps. Truly, the variety of intimacies possible between a man and a woman seemed to me almost beyond imagining, especially in our depleted state, and I wondered whether I'd live long enough ever to taste the fruit from this Tree of Knowledge.

While we stood and gawked, and came back for yet another fascinated look, a second promoter sidled up and, without the least embarrassment, let on that for only one ruble one could have the "full use" of a woman.

Glasnik and I looked around at these Cathayans with their smooth faces and pigtails and skirts, and, although our pockets were full of money we'd had no chance to spend all these months, I was damned if I could tell which was a woman and which was a man.

The pimp continued to tug at my elbow, and I couldn't decide. In fact, I found myself appealing to Heaven to restore my long-forgotten *yetzer hora* (inclination to sin). After all, I reasoned, here I was in the midst of a great and terrible war, and who knew if I would ever get back alive. Let me at least have this one experience before I died.

But I couldn't seem to summon up the necessary lust.

Meanwhile, other Russian soldiers came out of this place, buttoning themselves and fairly bursting with satisfaction.

Glasnik and I exchanged yet another uncertain look. I saw it was a mistake for us to come here together, because, frankly, we were both a little ashamed in front of each other. But in the end, with a bit of rough nudging from our gentile comrades, we all went inside. The pimp followed, rubbing his hands in anticipation.

There, in a dim room without a floor or furniture, the first thing I saw was a creature in Chinese trousers and a kind of short kaftan, who gave me a broad wink.

One of the Russian boys nudged me and said, "This one's yours." But I found I was unable to make a move.

After a few more drinks, though, we all began to relax a little more, our eyes became accustomed to the gloom, and I realized there were actually some fine-looking women there. Even the creature who winked at me now opened her jacket slightly and proved definitely not to be a man. I waited and waited for my poor neglected *yetzer hora* to be restored to me for at least a few moments. Meanwhile, some of my comrades continued to disappear into small adjoining cubicles shielded by ragged curtains which left very little to the imagination.

The schnapps, in truth, tasted like a mixture of sulfur and

rotten eggs. But it did have the power to make you drunk very quickly, and I kept refilling my glass, still hoping for desire to sweep me off my feet.

The Chinese person who had winked at me before now simply took my hand and drew me firmly into a windowless room. It was furnished only with a kind of mattress made of bamboo sticks.

Waiting for me to make a move, she daubed her face and whitened it with powder, which, I took it, was meant to make her more alluring. I stared at her more closely and, although I was almost totally anesthetized from what I'd drunk, I realized she smelled even worse than the schnapps. The closest I can describe it is a cellar full of onions which, over the winter, have begun to turn black and to disintegrate like corpses.

Now she crinkled her eyes at me and made inviting little gestures with her hands. I pantomimed with my hands and feet that I didn't feel quite ready yet and, in fact, hadn't actually made up my mind.

Her gestures grew more explicit, more coarse. The slender exotic flower was beginning to look to me more like a typical Petersburg whore, the kind once known by the expression *oifes t'mayim* ("unclean fowl").

I continued to sip at the vile stuff in my glass, to endow myself either with lust or else with the courage to walk out. To gain time, I told her I still didn't believe she was a woman.

She seemed to understand me perfectly and, with a great show of girlish modesty, she tightened the greasy curtain, then slowly removed her garment. What she put on display was a grimy, yellowish body which, without question, had all the necessary furnishings of a female. But, despite all I'd drunk, I was flooded with a sense of pure revulsion. I ripped aside the curtain and rushed out.

Glasnik joined me in the street. He could tell by my look that I had not been satisfied. But now the pimp and another gigantic

Cathayan came running out after me, demanding payment for the woman.

This struck me as so totally unreasonable that when the big Cathayan suddenly flashed a knife in his hands, I got angry and drew my revolver and made a threatening move at them. At this, apparently in fear of being robbed, they didn't merely return to their house of joy, but started to take off down the street with piercing cries of indignation.

And so, still faced with the bleak prospect of dying without ever having known the full taste of a woman, we supported one another as we staggered back to our camp.

The next morning I didn't feel virtuous so much as deathly ill. I bitterly reproached myself for having gone out with such frivolous and disgusting intentions, while my parents were living in a torment of uncertainty about the fate of their two youngest sons. In fact, either the Chinese schnapps or my revulsion at my weakness of character left me too sick to eat for several days and too feeble to drill my platoon, who, I'm sure, without any malice, would have been quite happy not to have me recover too soon.

Glasnik finally dragged me to the aid-station, where they gave me some repulsive white powder to swallow with water. I found out here from a wounded officer that, contrary to what we'd been told, Mukden had in fact already fallen, with the loss (to us) of some 200,000 men. And that, back home, there had been another unsuccessful attempt to assassinate the Czar, and, as usual, the wrong people had ended up suffering the consequences.

We asked the officer what chances he believed there were that the Czar would now agree to a negotiated peace. He was pessimistic. We had, of course, already lost the war. But the longer our Little Father kept us fighting, the longer he hoped to delay the revolution.

Back in our company sector, I was cheered to find there'd been another shipment of mail, although, once more, most of the

people to whom it was addressed would never answer to their
names again.

I had a fresh letter from my father. This time it was addressed
to me alone. My heart pounded as I tore it open. He wrote:

This is the seventeenth letter to which you have not replied. Your mother
is almost blinded with weeping. My dear child Jacob, I must also tell you
that I heard Avrohom is dead. However, the Gerer Rebbe specifically
assured me that you are alive and that you will, with the help of the
Almighty, return to us. Today I got up from sitting *shiva* for your brother,
may he dwell in a bright Eden. Your mother cries that her prayers were
insufficient to save him, and that he has not come to a Jewish grave. I
plead with her to regain her strength, so that she may live to see you and
your other brothers come back to us in a good hour.

Choked with bitterness, I told Glasnik that Avrohom was
dead. Therefore I now intended to keep my end of the bargain,
which was not to return without him.

Glasnik, seeing I was serious, argued angrily that the fact that
my father sat *shiva* was wholly insufficient proof that my brother
was actually dead. Assuming Avrohom were married, would there
not have had to be two eyewitnesses to his death before his wife
could be declared a widow?

For once, I had no patience with this Babylonian kind of
logic. In fact, ready to do the job before Glasnik, with his superior
knowledge of talmudic law, could weaken my resolve, I fumbled
for my revolver.

Glasnik looked at the weapon and shook his head. He wanted
to know, did I really want to be buried here, in the alien soil of
Cathay, where no one would ever be able to find my grave? Was
my determination so feeble that I was afraid I'd change my mind
if I waited merely until we got to a town large enough to have a
Jewish cemetery, where I'd be able at least to receive a proper
Jewish burial? Glasnik promised, if I'd agree to wait and kill myself
like a proper God-fearing Jew, he personally would dig my grave

and say *kaddish* for me. In fact, if the conditions were attractive enough, he might even decide to keep me company and shoot himself as well.

It took me some moments to realize he was joking, as usual. But suddenly, in dead earnest, he said, "Brother, we belong to the nation of Israel, and we have survived far worse than this, and by the merits of our holy ancestors and the tears of our parents, you'll see, we *will*, with His help, return alive."

I looked at him and felt moved to tears. What a gift it was to have a true friend! He now tried to cheer me up by picturing our homecoming, two young men straight as arrows, whom the most beautiful girls in our district would consider it a privilege to look upon; and the matchmakers would fall upon us like horseflies on a dung heap, but we would merely twirl our mustaches, and if they asked how much of a dowry we demanded, we'd tell them not to come back and talk to us about anything less than a thousand rubles.

So, thanks to Glasnik's eloquence, I didn't shoot myself that day.

A few mornings later, in the midst of a blinding snowstorm, I saw five horsemen approach our camp and beg for a bite to eat. I noticed the insignias on their uniforms. My heart stopped. They were from the Third Company, First Novocherkassky Regiment, Avrohom's unit.

I asked if they knew a soldier named Marateck.

They'd never heard the name. I turned away, crushed. But one of the horsemen explained they'd only been with the company for two days, and this gave me a moment of renewed hope. Until the second one said he knew there were hardly any men left of the original company. On the other hand, if I wanted to see for myself, they were stationed only about ten or twenty kilometers away.

I wrote down whatever directions they could give me, which wasn't much, since they themselves were lost. I ran to tell Glasnik I was going at once to find out for certain whether or not my brother was dead.

He argued with me that, despite all the rumors of peace negotiations, there were still Japanese snipers believed to be positioned on at least one of the hills I would have to pass. (This the horsemen had also confirmed.) Further, even if I managed to get past them, a lone Russian rider was almost certain to be ambushed by some roving band of Chinese highwaymen, especially at night.

I asked Glasnik and my friends Grabasz and Levandovski if they would come with me. They told me I was out of my mind. Glasnik pointed out it was literally not safe even to leave our camp for a small distance to answer a call of nature. Time and again our soldiers had been found shot with their trousers still about their ankles. In fact, just the night before, despite the guards we had posted all around, a Russian soldier was found with his belly slit open.

Levandovski begged me to forget my brother; no Jew or gentile had ever come back from the Eternal Place, and they absolutely refused to let me go on such a dangerous and useless journey.

As a final argument, they pointed out that the snow outside the camp was almost belly-high to a horse, and even in what little shelter we had, the icy wind cut through you like a razor.

I told them that suited me fine. Surely in such uncivilized weather, any sensible sniper or bandit would be huddling deep inside his cave, and I would have a much better chance of slipping past them.

The Russian soldier in charge of the horses was an old friend, whom I sometimes used to take with me to the synagogue in Petersburg on Friday night where, thanks to the generosity of the Jewish community, and in particular the legendary Baron Guinzburg ("the Russian Rothschild"), we were always rewarded afterwards with a sumptuous meal. This soldier not only enjoyed the food as much as any Jew, but wondered bitterly why his fellow Russians did not take such devoted care of *their* soldiers.

He advised me now not to take a horse but a mule, which

might go more slowly, but, under these terrible conditions, would have much better staying power.

My friends had given up trying to dissuade me. They handed over some of their own spare ammunition, and I left loaded down with a rifle, 120 rounds, a cavalry saber, and my revolver. Before leaving, I gave Glasnik my diary and begged him, if I didn't come back, to send it to my parents as a remembrance.

Based on what the lost horsemen from the Third Company had told me, I drew myself a rough map, which I tucked into the top of my boot. They'd also given me the password. It was "Red Girl."

Flurries of snow whipped my face as I climbed into the saddle and the mule carried me into the night.

By my watch, it was barely 8:30. The ten or twenty kilometers, even under these conditions, should not take more than three hours. Whether or not I would try to return tonight depended of course on how much danger I encountered en route, but, above all, on the kind of news I got when I arrived.

Three hours later, I found myself in the midst of an endless forest. It had stopped snowing and, despite my fear of bandits, I struck a match to consult my map. If the map was even roughly accurate, I had covered less than half the distance. After emerging from the forest, *if* I came out at the right spot, I would still have to climb a considerable hill, then cross a body of water which might or might not be a river, and might or might not be frozen over.

Now that the snow had ceased, the moon fell upon me like a searchlight. Not only was I easily visible to every bandit in China, but the noise made by my mule surely must have carried for miles. I held the bridle in one hand and my revolver in the other. The trees bent and groaned under the weight of the snow, each one of them a perfect hiding place for a Cathayan bandit, whom the value of my weapons alone, not to mention the mule, would keep in luxury for half a year.

By the time I got through the forest and reached the edge of the water, it was long past one in the morning. Fortunately, my friends had also insisted on supplying me with some dry rusks and an onion, which I consumed like a fire and washed down with a long gulp from a small bottle of the rank Chinese liquor they'd provided.

About to hang a bag of oats under the snout of my exhausted mule, it struck me anew that, out here in the open, even a blind man could pick me off on the first shot. The food stuck in my throat, and I urged my mule to hurry across the ice.

I was able now to see the outlines of a ruined hut on the opposite shore. Its roofless walls might, unless inhabited by Heaven-knows-who, give us a sheltered place to rest for a while.

Meanwhile, the mule's clumsy hooves had cracked the ice, and suddenly there was no more ice, and the mule, unable to halt in time, skidded and stumbled headlong and spilled me into the frozen water. Fortunately, the river or lake here was only neck-deep. But as we emerged on the opposite shore, I was shivering like a leaf in a high wind, and the mule behaved as though it was having a fit.

I put the bottle to my mouth, but my fall had broken it, and I was able to extract only a mouthful of foul, alcoholic fumes. The clothes began to stiffen on my body, my head boiled with fever, I felt myself grow dizzy and, for good measure, my vision began to blur. As for my feet, they were as responsive as two blocks of granite. I said to myself, "Master of the Universe, have I come through all these hardships and dangers only to die here, where no Jew will ever find my body?"

The mule, in the meantime, already seemed to have recovered from its fit, and was nibbling thoughtfully at the immaculate snow. With some difficulty, I climbed up on its back again. My clothes were as cold and hard as a suit of armor. I tried to thrust my feet into the stirrups, but found I had to raise them or they'd drag in the snow. Each foot weighed a ton and I decided perhaps it was just as well that I couldn't feel them any longer. In fact, to be quite truthful, I had begun to regret I didn't listen to my friends.

To make sure I had enough on my mind, the mule now cheerfully blundered into a snowbank so deep that he would be there to this day if I hadn't dismounted and, walking on the two lumps of ice in my boots, tried to pull him back out.

I was still trying to reach the ruined hut, which seemed to me no closer than it had an hour ago. Assuming no one was there, I had every intention of lying down for a while, even at the risk of falling asleep and turning into something that could stand comparison with Lot's wife.

But just as I reached the ruined hut, another blow fell. I saw from my new point of vantage that, beyond the hut, there were at least half a dozen possible paths. I consulted my frozen map. There was nothing whatever on it to correspond to this tangle of roads. In the morning, even if I did wake up and regain my strength, how would I know which path to choose?

A ravenous howl broke the silence behind me. I suddenly realized I was surrounded by wolves. I quickly dragged the mule into the ruined hut. Together we took up a defensive position in one of the corners. I drew my revolver and held it in readiness to defend us against the sudden flash of a jaw leaping at us out of the darkness. In that heroic position, as day broke, I fell asleep.

Again, I seemed able only to dream of the dead. But this time I felt as awed as our father Jacob, on the road from Beersheba to Horon, must have felt when the angel spoke to him, saying, "I will not abandon you." For, in this dream, my grandfather, Reb Shmuel Schlossberg, of blessed memory, appeared to me, bearing in his hands a red clay vessel covered with white linen.

Exactly as in my childhood, he seemed to have come in response to my moans of distress and, in his customary way, he asked, "What is it, my child?"

I cried, *"Zayde*, I'm dying," and broke into tears.

He stroked my cheek and said, "You will not die," and he had me drink from the clay vessel in his hands.

As I drank, endlessly, feeling no need to pause for breath, he said, "If you will take the second road to the left of the hill, you will find your brother." He even advised me where I would locate my mule, which I hadn't realized was lost.

I awakened, startled to find it was night, although probably the following night. I must have been asleep for close to twenty hours. The mule was gone.

For some moments I still looked for my grandfather, in order to continue our conversation. Gradually, I realized it was a dream and I was now either awake or else had plunged into a new nightmare, in which I was lost in the snows of Cathay. But it seemed to have gotten warmer, and my long sleep had left me feeling refreshed and, strangely, once more full of hope.

But a moment later I realized I could not for the life of me recall where my grandfather told me to look for the mule. But never mind. Even if it meant continuing on foot, I was determined to follow his advice and take "the second road to the left of the hill," although I could not really picture what he meant by that.

When I came to the road I *thought* my grandfather had told me to take, I suddenly found my mule. The creature was calmly eating snow, as though to leave me in no doubt that my difficulties were none of *his* concern.

I was filled now with an unshakable conviction that if my grandfather knew exactly where I'd find my mule, why would he not also be right about my brother?

Mounted once again, I carefully pursued the path Reb Shmuel had instructed me to take. But after some time, the moon abruptly ducked behind a cloud and I was left surrounded by a wall of impenetrable darkness. Could my dream have deceived me after all?

Before I gave way to despair, it occurred to me that, so close to the enemy, a Russian encampment of course would not be permitted to light fires at night. And almost as soon as my eyes became accustomed to the darkness, it seemed to me that I saw moving figures and even heard an occasional voice.

I had to force myself to remain skeptical, as well as on my guard. I have always believed in dreams, and I have no doubt that the dead know things that are hidden from the living. Yet how could my grandfather possibly have known my brother's address in darkest Manchuria? With a burst of impatience, I virtually galloped downhill toward the camp and almost got shot. I saw the sentry only when his rifle was already tracking me and, as I managed to halt my mule, the password fled from my mind.

The sentry threatened to fire.

"Do I sound like a Japanese?" I asked him.

He said he had his orders and began to count to three.

A little later than the last moment, I cried out, "Red Girl!"

The sentry reluctantly decided not to shoot me. I asked him about the Third Novocherkassky Company. He hesitated, because the Japanese were known to be using some Polish spies and he was convinced, no doubt correctly, that our own army didn't even know of the existence of this camp, because they had received neither replacements nor mail, let alone provisions, and thus had been forced to subsist entirely by foraging.

But in the end he decided to trust me and told me that what was left of the Third Company was here, and he pointed out to me where I'd find them.

In the dim moonlight, I recognized the caps worn by my brother's unit. But all the faces were strange to me. It was clear that all *my* acquaintances were long dead.

My heart beating unbearably, I ran from one group of figures to the next. Most were still awake, but none had ever heard of my brother.

I finally encountered a familiar face, a German boy named Friedrich Vogel, a notorious jokester, who'd been part of the original company. He was carrying an empty pail, on his way to fetch water. When he saw me, he cried, "Marateck!" and dropped the pail.

I looked at him more closely. He looked aged by a good twenty years. Only his squeaky voice was still the same. Meanwhile, he had recovered from his fright and forced a smile, to show I hadn't really frightened him, that he was only joking.

Without any greeting, I demanded, "Is my brother still alive?"

"Who?"

"My *brother!*" I shouted at him. "Marateck!"

"Your brother," he said. "Ah. Didn't you know?" He made a long face. "Somebody else is already walking in his boots."

"He's *dead?*" I cried out, and all the strength went out of me. So my grandfather's appearance in my dream was simply a cruel mockery. But of course he hadn't actually said I would find Avrohom alive.

The German watched me with open curiosity and finally said, *"He* thought all along it was *you* who were dead." He seized my arm. "Come, you'll see your brother."

"You mean he's buried *here?*"

At which the damned German gave me a nudge and said, "Couldn't you tell I was joking? I only said somebody is wearing his boots. In fact, he and I just killed a goat, to celebrate the end of the war. I was just getting water for tea."

I felt my feet doing a little dance, and instantly forgave the German for his German sense of humor, a talent someone wiser than I once described as "no laughing matter." In fact, I begged him to keep quiet now and let me surprise my brother.

Moments later, still hidden, I saw Avrohom and a few other good old friends eating large chunks of boiled goat meat, smoking their pipes, and even passing around a clear bottle of something that didn't seem to be water. My brother, too, looked changed, aged, and not really healthy. But then, I hadn't looked at myself lately.

For some time I listened to them cosily chatting about girls, a subject of which they knew even less than I, and about the rumor that America, to save Russian pride, finally had helped both sides arrange an end to the war.

I stood in the darkness until I saw pain clouding Avrohom's face for a moment, and he said, "Ah, if my brother Yankel were alive, what a celebration we'd have now." Tears filled my eyes, and I suddenly felt choked and ashamed as I burst out of the darkness and cried, "Here I am!"

For a moment or two, he seemed to believe I was either some sort of a demon, or his friend's idea of a bad joke. His eyes had a haunted, feverish look. Half-smiling, half-crying, I quoted to him from the *Shabbos* morning Psalms, *"Yipoil mitzidcho elef . . ."* ("A thousand may fall at your side, and ten thousand at your right hand, yet it shall not come near you").

Still silent, he finally nodded and shyly offered me the piece of meat he was holding in his hand. Only when I embraced him did he permit himself to relax and believe I was actually alive.

All the rest of that night, until daybreak, we sat and talked and laughed and ate and resolutely got drunk. By morning, Avrohom was able even to joke about the silly misunderstanding which had convinced him *I* was dead. Now he only hoped our postal service had remained faithful to its traditions and lost the letter in which he had let my parents know I'd been killed in action.

After all, he said, if, after having already sat *shiva* for *him*, our parents now also had gone into mourning for me (not to mention the time I had once before returned from the Other World), they would by now be such experienced *shiva*-sitters, they could go into business as professional mourners.

And so drunk and hysterical were we at that moment, we thought even *that* was funny.